A Passion for Compassion

A Passion for Compassion

while Dancing Through Our Light A Lamplighters Guide

Volume I

Sita Paloma

Waterside Productions

Copyright © 2024 by Sita Paloma

All rights reserved. This book or any portion thereof may not be reproduced or used in any manner whatsoever without the express written permission of the publisher except for the use of brief quotations in articles and book reviews.

NO AI TRAINING: Without in any way limiting the author's [and publisher's] exclusive rights under copyright, any use of this publication to "train" generative artificial intelligence (AI) technologies to generate text is expressly prohibited. The author reserves all rights to license uses of this work for generative AI training and development of machine learning language models.

First Printing, 2024

ISBN-13: 978-1-962984-37-9 print edition
ISBN-13: 978-1-962984-38-6 e-book edition

Waterside Productions
2055 Oxford Ave
Cardiff, CA 92007
www.waterside.com

This Book is Dedicated to All Children, Young and Old

Contents

Introduction

My wish is to write a lullaby — XI
How Best to Use This Guide — XIII

Part I

1   **Chapter One**   *A Debut* — 3
...feeling the sweet secret circle... — 4
Now as One Who is Waking Up — 5
I Do Slow — 5
Lamplighter — 7
9/11 — 8

2   **Chapter Two**   *A Long Time Ago* — 11
A Visit by Our Lovely Dear Buddha — 12
The Year Was 1999

3   **Chapter Three**   *How little faith I had back then.* — 19
One Day Long Ago — 20
Proof To Me — 21
Who Am I? Who Are You? — 22

Part II

4   **Chapter Four**   *What's It All About?* — 27
So What Is It All About? — 27
Hey Sam — 28

5   **Chapter Five**   *Let's Check This Out* — 31
Some Pearls of Wisdom — 31
The Big Deal - For attitude adjustment — 31
Then there is our monkey mind. — 32
A Place of Warmth — 32
What Am I Really Thinking? Becoming Aware — 32

	Pearl of Wisdom	*33*
	Connecting is our first step	
	Driving	34
	Dear Lamplighter	*36*
	We Pray	*36*
6	**Chapter Six** NEEDS	39
	Let us differentiate between need and needy.	*40*
	The Need is the Key We Need	41
	Hidden Agenda	42
	Figuring out my need	43
	Pearl of Wisdom, Confidence	*43*
	Soul Connection is the Expansion	*44*
	Daily Menu	45
	Dear Lord	*46*
7	**Chapter Seven** *Connecting*	49
	3-D God web	50
	Real Connection Beyond Our Wildest Dreams	51
	Thank You Dear Lord	*54*
8	**Chapter Eight** *Feelings*	57
	A Lamplighters Guide to Soul Communication	*57*
	Rationalizing	58
	Our Primary and Basic Personal Need	60
	Expressions and Explosive Tears	*61*
	Vulnerability	62
	Can we ever know?	*65*
9	**Chapter Nine** *Spiritual Needs*	67
	A Little Movie	*67*
	Becoming Aware of Personal Spiritual Needs	68
	Open the Window	*71*
	No Doubt	*71*
10	**Chapter Ten** *Happiness*	73
	Pearls of Wisdom	*74*
	May We Be	*75*
	Dear Lamplighter	*75*
11	**Chapter Eleven** *Connecting the Dots*	79
	One Day	*79*

Vortex   *81*
Pearls of Wisdom   *83*
Thank you Dear Lord   *84*

Part III

12   **Chapter Twelve** *The Art of Passion for Compassion*   89
Hidden agendas - ha!   89
Mercy Mercy   90
Turn on the Light, Please   91
We <u>can</u> work with our emotions   92
Let's talk about this.   93
The first point. <u>I told a lie to myself</u>.   93
The second point. <u>Interpretations</u>   94
The Real Truth Is   94
Pearl of Wisdom   95
The third point. <u>Hidden Agendas</u>. <u>Ha</u>!   96
Pearl of Wisdom   97
May I?   98

13   **Chapter Thirteen** *What Ambiance Do I Want?*   101
Self Empathy is a shift of consciousness we need   102
A Little Addition   103
To be real   104
A Prayer   105

14   **Chapter Fourteen**
Capture the Ability to Feel What I Wanna Feel   107
La Novela   107
What's Up   109

15   **Chapter Fifteen**   Fourth Point, <u>Label</u>   111
When we truly dance, we just dance.
Without accusations or expectations   112

16   **Chapter Sixteen** *Searching For Truth*   115
Sweet Mantra   116
Help Us   117

17   **Chapter Seventeen** *Practicing the Dance*   119
The Appetite   119

	How to Practice this New Dance: Developing Two Important Steps	120
	Pearls of Wisdom	*122*
18	**Chapter Eighteen** Obliging and the Middle Path	125
	The power in differentiating thoughts from feelings	126
	Seeking the Middle Road	*127*
	How About That?	*128*
19	**Chapter Nineteen** Suggestions for a New Vortex	*131*

Part IV

20	**Chapter Twenty** The Embodiment of Compassion	135
	A Sweet Story	*135*
	Pearl of Wisdom	*137*
	Owning the Choice to Hear	138
	Yes Yes!	*138*
21	**Chapter Twenty One** Let's Talk About Love	*141*
	La *Chirimoya Metals*	*141*
	Acceptance, Acceptance, Acceptance, with Passion	*142*
	This is a Big Deal!	*142*
	In Summary	*143*
22	**Chapter Twenty Two** *a little truth*	145

Part V

23	**Chapter Twenty Three A Lamplighter's Guide**	**149**
	The gateway to communicating with our souls	149
	A Little Story	*150*
	I Pray Today	*151*
	Steps to Our Soul Journey	152
	A list of some emotions we feel:	
	when our needs are met :-)	153
	when our needs are not being met :-(	154

Acknowledgements	157
Photos	159

Introduction

My wish is to write a lullaby.

Something new is coming.
We need soothing.
We need help.
A shift is happening.
In each of us and in our world.
We question, "Who are we really? What's really going on?"

This is a guide for us. A guiding lullaby for our paths to soul communications. A guiding lullaby in uniting our heart, soul and mind connections. Ridding us of shame, guilt and the disorganized ego.

Could it then be, it's time for us to become *loving lamplighters*?

What is a lamplighter?
Simply, a lamplighter is a person who helps to light our lamps, that light in each of us.

This guiding lullaby is about lighting our lamps, young and old, active and inactive, searching and knowing. A guide using stories, pearls of wisdom, poetry and prose; tools for expressing and living compassionately. Offering a life full of love and peace, no matter what the circumstances are.

By sharing my story, how my life and world had a shift in dimensional consciousness, along with offering pearls of wisdom given to me, I hope to direct our consciousness into a magical, mystical whirlwind of joy and peace, passing on our light of love.

May I rock 'n cradle you as you read through this guide and light our lamps ever more.

How Best to Use This Guide

Read it all the way through. Or read it several times all the way through.

There may be new information you'd like to think about and ponder.

Ponder for a minute or two...

The suggestion is to then read on. Do not stop. Just read on.

This guiding lullaby is a soul journey. Step by step, chapter by chapter, poem by poem, pearls of wisdom; allow the words to flow.

Allow yourself to be cradled anew.

Take your time reading... an afternoon, a week's time or more.

Allow sleep and dream time to also play their role.

May you enjoy reading this guiding lullaby all the way through.

May your lamp be ever lit, may your love and compassion overflow. With love, Sita Paloma

Part I

Part 1

Chapter One

A Debut

As a child, a passion began to grow in me, for exploring, expressing and pretending....

One day, as I ventured through some tall willow reeds, I found a small circular spot of reeds flattened. How excited was I! I thought it a hidden secret. I sat, then lay flat, surrounded by tall, straight, green skinny plants. I could feel a tunnel of bright light coming through to my little found circle, warming me and my secret spot.

Later that year, a little secret princess, me, I thought, was about to have her debut.

……… Hardly anyone knew who she was. They thought she was an extra-quiet child, not aware, without a care. She knew better to hide from them. They were confused. But that passion needed to emerge and express the hidden secret of the delight that may be.

She waited silently for that momentous moment of first note, sounding out "Get ready!" Then rhythm in tune with music sound, she bounced out on stage, a little tiny fairy princess.

She was dressed in a billowing white dress with thin red trim and a red velvety vest, tied true gypsy style, with red velvet ribbon, criss cross across her chest, with the ends of the ribbon dangling.

There, too, with smile huge, the little girl knew for one minute or two that she could transform the onlookers' lives into a storybook page of sound, animation and joy. For she felt high knowing too, her added foot tapping and castanets would take the joyous dance to a field of fun 'n play……….

…. As I stood and prepared in my silence, suddenly, there on the stage up high, I was *feeling the sweet secret circle* once again. A little circus of fun it was, with its tunnel of warm light, circling around and about, giving the delight I had once found, in the spot of flattened reeds.

Stepping out, whirling about, making sure all could see the billowing of my pretty dress, I could only see their eyes waiting, yearning too, ready to receive a gift I so graciously wanted to give.

Then I could feel the *warm secret light was circling around, reaching out to touch us all.* This encouraged my pretending.

Centering myself on stage, I performed the steps practiced true. Each tap was heard clearly in perfect tune. Arms raised low and high in harmony with steps and song. I smiled huge, a glamorous red....

Sita Paloma

Looking out I saw clearly a woman dear, whose eyes were fixated on my every move, encouraging me even more with her admiration. I then felt full of confidence and knew for sure, my performance was in proper tune to connect with my audience.

Realizing then, we could all be now, within that circle of sweetness, feeling and sharing... for a minute or two, the *light in the delight* of my little tiny secret circle. This made me feel complete and grand!

****

Although I had the *warm light* deep within me, in school it was hard to find a friend. I didn't think I could possibly be different from any other child, but little by little was told so. I was separated for various reasons I did not understand. The children at play only knew I was to be ignored. This made me sad.

Also I was confused for I knew true, deep down within my tiny being, that I could not be different, that each one of us is an extra-ordinary person, just looking for fun and happiness. And I just wanted to meet the kids and have fun, figuring we all had the passion for adventure.

Little by little I did begin to see what my world was all about. Many restrictions were the norm. I yearned for freedom, for I knew what freedom was. I had experienced it, when in the *light of the delight*, and it felt fine.

Now as One Who is Waking Up

Looking back I can clearly see that every child must come into the world with a passion for exploring, expressing and then pretending....

Dear Reader, Dear Dear Lamplighter, I'd like to ask you.... I'd like to hear all about a time when you think you might have had your very own debut; an adventure, a *coming-out* to, or going *inward* within, while maintaining the understanding that there's an outside world. Yet knowing something, or acknowledging something special deep within you.... A special time that you think your persona might have been acknowledging your soul: a soul debut?   How about that?

And now.... may I please share a poem I wrote as the forward to this book? Thinking of myself as someone who may write something for others to read, has been odd. Therefore a need I have is for further explanation of who I am.

The poem was the result of a fear within that I may be criticized for my non-writing skills. I tried giving my editor reasons why I am, why I write. She insisted proper commas, dots and spaces be applied. Also some reversing and asked, "*What does that mean?*" "*Aha!*" I answered, "*I wondered myself, 'what does that mean?'*"

I Do Slow

I am slow.
I talk slow.
I move slowly.
My knowledge comes to me
slowly.

Having been told I am dyslexic.
Having been told I confuse my listeners
as I am confused,
mixing Spanish and English sentence
structure.

Having been told I am a little backwards.

But....... those telling me
what I am, to me, have been odd.
To me their view is *one* only.
My mind has a hard time with that.

Expansion is my mind.
Expansion I hope I may
This Life Enjoy.

Curiosity is my name.
Named so by Nancy Ann
Tappe, tapping into my inner wilderness.
Thank you.

Later then .... if I did not have enough proof of
confusing my audience such,
Was told by another:
"*Oh honey dear,
your astrological natal chart dictates
you have
Mercury retrograde
always.*"

What I may add is this:

Sita Paloma

Tho they tried to confuse me,
Even said "you are a slow and maybe dumb child,
cannot read, cannot learn,
we may need to hold you back."

When introduced to numbers and order
I had no challenge
Only fun, like crosswords for some.

Tho this seemed to anger them
anyway
It taught me I had no problem with order.
And then knew I was not the
One confused.

Though I did have a problem
throughout my early life,
being forced to sit
agonizing hours,
Knowing True,
my youth wasting
on gibberish.

Now grown 65 wise.
Anyone I meet
can recognize,
a soul worthwhile
their time to stop
and converse,
if nothing more
than feeling touched by
One Willing
Now to Hold the
Flame to *their*
worthiness.

So now I write
in poetry.
For they told me
structure obtrusive
holds no power there.
I sigh in relief.

What Soul & Mind
Wonderings
Shall I encounter?
Maybe a page, a
troll or fairy
may wander thru
relaying a message
or two for you 'n me
As we two for now
Won the Power
of *One.*

We are One,
One People
One Race,
The Human Race.
Well maybe
just maybe
we are One too
With those little creatures
we call friends.
Those little sometimes big
fuzzy little creatures.
True friends they are…..

Lamplighter

*O*ne *D*ay, I was anxiously waiting for Phyllis Krystal to come up on stage. She was holding a one-day workshop on her book *"Cutting the Ties that Bind"*.

Although I had not read her book, I liked the title.

During the question-and-answer period, I stood and asked a question on her use of the word "obliging". After she explained her use of the word, I must have sat down with still an expression of confusion.

Then during break time, as I was helping myself to some tea and cookies, I felt a slight tap on my right shoulder. Turning around, I found a delightfully happy woman saying that she'd noticed my expression of confusion even after Phillis gave her explanation, and she offered to give me further explanation.

Joyfully I accepted her offer with open arms and yet some curiosity. I wondered if she had been especially sent to me.

With a twinkle in her eyes, she completed her pearls of wisdom by saying, *"You know... we lamplighters need to get it right."*

She then paused, and looked deeply into my eyes with such love and compassion. I'd never heard the expression *lamplighters* before, and yet, this term resonated in me so wonderfully that I now knew for sure, she had been especially sent to me.

She then disappeared into the crowd. I never got her name.

Sita Paloma

9/11

Then one day I had an unusual healing experience. I woke up early with the phone ringing. Thinking something must be up, I answered it.

A friend told me to turn on the television immediately.

Turning on the TV, I watched the twin towers in New York City crumble down. It was September 11th, 2001.

With understanding what was taking place, I immediately felt fear. Scary thoughts were going through me. I felt terrified for the folks in the twin towers and fear for our world.

What could I do? I decided I needed to talk to God, so I sat in meditation, asking God to give me whatever information I may need, right now.

It took me a while to get in the state of meditation because of my fearful monkey mind. Finally, I was able to sink into a deep meditation.

After a while I received a pleasing, beautiful warm vision.

A view of the entire world appeared. It was round and large, full of color and it felt very much alive and active! Like it was breathing! It was gorgeous, peaceful and complete.

Then, the entire planet became dark. It was not dark because it was night time. No, because the entire world was dark. Almost as if life was being shut down.

Suddenly a few lights, like little stars, lit up here and there on a continent. Slowly but surely more lights began to sparkle here and there.

The world then slowly turned, showing more little tiny star lights that were beginning to flicker on.

After some time, I realized each light was a planet caregiver. Each light was a person who was working to light the lamps around the world and bring back life! Once lit, the light would be permanent!

At that moment, I received a gift of great relief! It seemed like relief and peace were surrounding my whole being!

With this sweet vision and healing, I became calm and happy. I then knew we would be okay. Somehow, some way, even through whatever sacrifices may arise, we are being protected, the world is being protected.

And... *lamplighters* are being called to light up the world. Plus they are being directed where and when to light a lamp!

Later that morning, I received another phone call. Someone was in need and was asking for a healing. Since I was a practicing healer, they hoped I could help. The 9/11 news was out and fear was rapidly growing. I felt calm.

For many weeks I continued to get alarming phone calls. All were looking for a healing.

Because of my beautiful morning gift, I was being guided as to how to help calm each person that called me. It was not difficult at all!

Little by little I came to realize that I was experiencing an initiation to become a *lamplighter*. Knowing where and when to help light a lamp. How about that?

****

How about your initiation *Dear Lamplighter*? How was it for you?
Or, how is it for you? Are you feeling an initiation now?
Hoping someday there is a time to share. ;-)

***

Chapter Two
A Long Time Ago

A long long time ago, some 20 plus years, I began to pave a new path for my life as I entered a world unknown. A world with God, angels and saints.

Though this may sound angelic, my known world began to crumble. I then began a search. Little by little, a bigger picture was shown to me and I saw how we are all connected.

Dear Fellow *Lamplighter*, I'd like to share a story with you that changed my life.

A little background is needed first.

My given name is Teresita Villaseñor. I was raised Catholic. I became a strong devotee early on. Then I began to question the teachings about God in the fifth grade when my teacher showed little concern for prayers that I was requesting. Assurance was needed that miracles could come true for my dear little friend, diagnosed with leukemia. Being the shy little girl and scared of adults by then, I waited until the end of the day to ask my teacher for her prayers. She never looked at me, only continued with her school chores. Her answer was that we do not know why the good Lord wants to take some so early.

In the few seconds it took me to hear her response, my world changed. What I heard her say was that miracles only happened during biblical times and that my friend would surely die. Also that she, my teacher, who was also a nun, the most holy and thoughtful person I had ever met, had no concern for anything that mattered to me. Though I prayed wholeheartedly, my friend did die. Little by little I began to question everything after that.

It was somewhat of a torturous affair to finally come to the decision a few years later that all the adults I knew were crazy and God could not exist; that he was a figment of their imagination. I declared myself an atheist.

But my internal torture did continue for years anyway, until I became a hippie. I had searched for a replacement. The hippie movement was all about love and accepted all people. I was in. The God question bothered me only a tad after that.

Then one day the hand of God, I like to tease, came down on earth and woke me up. A few years later, I had this dream.

A Visit by Our Lovely Dear Buddha
The Year Was 1999

Upon waking one day, feeling wonderful, refreshed and full of subtle mischief, I thought I had had a dream. I was simply intrigued by my memory of it. Totally fixated on the details of the beautiful dream, I had to relive it.

Sitting on the beach, my legs stretched out, leaning back on my arms and hands, I was looking up to the warm sun with eyes closed.

Wearing modern clothes, I sat in knee length pants and a simple white, sleeveless blouse. I was in my late-40s. The waters were sitting softly on the edge of the shore.

Suddenly I heard some mumbling to the left and so I looked over. A young man was approaching me. He was upset, carrying a silver briefcase which was looking important. It did not have a lock on it.

The bright sky above him was a pleasant sky blue. However, in the far far distance behind him, I could see a castle type building which sprawled out. It was extremely far, as if in another time. It was surrounded by some fog and low grayish clouds.

He was a handsome young man, stylish. Maybe 15 or 16 years old, dressed in attire from a time long lost.

While remembering the dream, I smiled, being amazed at how vivid the details were of his hair and clothing.

He was wearing a flowing outfit, pants and shirt. They were in shades of grey, light and dark, natural colors, 100% silk, even the sewing threads. Most of the outfit was a soft, light color of gray with the trim almost black. About a 2 inch trim outlined the long shirt around the bottom edge and up the center. It was then buttoned-up with beautiful cloth buttons, and loops to close it up. The sleeves were long and flowing with the same dark trim. The pants were the soft light gray.

He had thick black hair, all pulled back straight and tight. The thick coarse hair was gathered up on top of his head, folded back and forth to make about a 5 - 6 inch bow like bundle, with some sort of clasp, midway through the folded hair. It was detailed and gorgeous! It was about 3 inches wide, making a rectangular shaped bow.

He looked Asian. His almond eyes showed he was upset. He was fed up with his life.

His skin was smooth and perfect -- not a wrinkle, not a blemish. Though he was frowning, his brow had no crinkle; the skin was perfect, fresh like a newborn baby. His eyebrows, thick eyelashes and hair were black black, giving a nice contrast and beauty to his light colored face.

He looked like walking art. He had high smooth cheekbones. His face was a little wide, almost square, yet his forehead and sweet rounded chin added to a more rectangular shaped head and face. He stood tall, slender and strong. Handsome does not describe his beauty. More like gorgeous.

As he walked, the flowing outfit had a smooth wave going through it. This allowed the light and dark colors of the outfit to dance a little. The movement gave a reflective highlight to the dark and light colors of his face. Maybe the sun was shining in a certain direction to offer the beautiful scene. This gave me the look of walking art. Absolutely stunning he was.

He was looking for someone he could give his briefcase to. He didn't want it any longer. He was tired of schooling.

As he had been mumbling, he finally spoke clearly, telling me of his woes and to take the briefcase. He didn't want the responsibility the briefcase represented and required. He did not want to do the work any longer. What work, I do not know.

I sat up tall, delighted to be offered such an important gift. But I argued with him, knowing the briefcase was not mine to be. It belonged to him; it took him years of schooling to get whatever was in the briefcase. As a mother I knew he'd need his education and notes.

He said no. He was totally defiant. I finally came to the conclusion that he wasn't going to change his mind but he really needed to chill. So I said, "Okay, but we'll do a trade. It'll take two years." He said, "Alright."

I then leaned over and out of my right pocket I pulled out a big wadded up ball of hash, the condensed sacred marijuana herb of the hemp plant. I handed it to him.

He was still standing and I was still sitting. He accepted the ball with his right hand.

His brow of anger dropped as it shifted to being perplexed. His anger had only surfaced for a few seconds.

As the young man accepted my gift, I added, "Take a tiny piece of this and eat it one time per day. You will know at what time to eat it." He nodded a yes.

Satisfied, the young man put the ball of hash into his right pocket and simply walked off to the left. But rather than retrace his steps back to the castle, he walked along the water shore for a while, then walked straight into a forest and disappeared.

Although he did not say goodbye, I thought our deal sealed as I watched him disappear, not coming back. Grateful for the deal and to have been the one in his path that day, I was left, still sitting in the same spot, in a state of total bliss.

I sat with briefcase in hand, simply intrigued and definitely overly anxious to see what was in the briefcase.

As I opened the briefcase, it turned into an old-fashioned traveling trunk. Like the trunk I played with as a child, which had belonged to my grandmother, doña Guadalupe.

The trunk was maybe 4 feet by 2 feet by 2 feet. Looking inside, there was a hook at the top center, so the half trunk could be a little tiny closet to hang clothes on.

On a hanger hung his outfit from his schooling days. It was a duplicate of what I saw him wearing but it was very old, becoming thin. The colors were not vibrant and fresh. The outfit had been washed and finely pressed; looking as if to preserve the reverence it held by the tailor and the ones who cared for it during the young man's schooling.

The other half turned back into the modern-day silver metal briefcase. As I opened it I noticed there were a whole bunch of files built into the case. Totally delighted, as if I had found a mystery inside a mystery, as I had never seen a briefcase with a built-in file cabinet. Intrigued again, delighted in my suspense to look through the files, I woke up.

When I woke up, I was so excited, I didn't really care that I didn't get to see what was in the files. A little curious, but my happiness was greater than my curiosity!

That day, my journey continued, with the Lord in the form of the sneaky Lord of Mystery, paving steps to lead me to more curiosity and ask, *"Now what's really going on? Is someone watching me?"*

I had planned to have lunch with a couple of girlfriends. One friend picked me up and was delighted to announce it was Wesak. Okay, what's that? She said it was the last Buddha full moon of the century and had special meaning.

We were to drive to the other friend's house when I remembered I needed to tell my brother something, who was on the way. My brother is always talking about something. So, when we arrived, he was as entertaining as usual. As I listened, his conversation reminded me of my beautiful morning dream. There was a need to share it and so I did.

When I finished my brother simply said, *"Oh that was Buddha. Buddha visited you."*
"What? Noooo, he was not fat. This was a very young man. He was a prince of some sort!"

"Yes!" my brother insisted. *"Buddha was a prince and he was young at one point!"*

And so we argued. He then said Buddha was Siddhartha. What? I thought Siddhartha was a sweet little novel which I never finished reading.

As we girlfriends continued on our journey to our friend's house, I felt perplexed. When we arrived, our friend greeted us warmly, giving us each a little tiny statue of a fat Happy Buddha. I could feel my eyebrows bending into a deep frown, becoming concerned. I asked myself, *"What is going on?"*

Compelled once again to share my dream, I simply spilled my story, repeating now in detail the whole dream without asking if I should. My friend looking deeply into my eyes, then with a grin, said, *"Wait a minute,"* as she held up one finger and left the room.

My friend returned with a large postcard of Buddha. The backside was divided into four. Each section had a picture with little-known information about Buddha. One corner had a picture of seeds, claiming Buddha lived off of hemp seeds during his isolated time in the forest.

Buddha spent time in a forest? Buddha was a real person?

My heart began to beat loudly. I began to have some fear with the idea that a dead master of some sort *could* visit me and why *would* he? Oh dear, oh my! Who am I?

The next day, Friday, I returned to massage school. I had been given a scholarship to my surprise and was told, *"Those are healing hands."* I looked at my hands and said, *"They are?"* not knowing all hands have the potential to heal.

So grateful was I. However, returning to school in my forties proved to be a challenge. Enjoying the process of learning something new, that Friday proved to expand my mind even more as my Buddha journey continued with the sneaky Lord of Mystery who was working with me!

There was one other fellow student who shared the returning to school. He was a bit older, a shiatsu master massage therapist from Japan. He spoke little English but could understand. He had heard of this school, IPSB, moved to Pacific Beach to enroll and learn all he could. So there he was in a beginning massage class.

During break time the master masseur would become surrounded by the younger male students wanting to converse.

On this Friday at break time I found myself sitting next to the sweet, holy-feeling Master. Realizing we sat alone, no students milling around him, I asked myself, *"Why is this happening?"* Assuming he knew about Buddha, I continued, *"Should I tell him my dream and ask if he thought it was Buddha visiting?"* I received an internal, *"Yes yes!"* So I asked if I could share my dream and get his opinion. He said yes.

I gave him all the details except for the trade. It was just too controversial for me at that time. After, he asked, *"What did the water look like?"* Surprised, I began to visualize my dream again. He then added, *"Were there any waves?"* Amazed, I realized there were none. He then asked, *"What color was the sand?"* Again surprised and dazzled with his question, I began to search my memory.

As I looked down, I was astonished to see that it did not look like our local beach sand. I had never paid much attention to the local sand before.

As the master helped me search the vision I realized our local beach has a brightness to it as the sand is fine, light in color and therefore reflects the sun more. This sand I saw was not the light blue grey tiny beads in southern California. It did not have the stark beaming reflection. The beach had a soft shine, somewhat gray-green in color. The grains of sand were larger, more of a flat speck rather than rounded bead.

The master, watching my reaction, listened intensely to my silence, beckoning me to share more. After some time I finally answered that no, it was not our local sand, the sand was not gray but more of a green, and the grains were larger, not tiny at all.

The master then jumped back, though we were still sitting on the classroom floor. His back arched backwards as if to get further away from me, to have greater room to throw his hands up in exasperation. Swinging one arm high up, he then quickly swung it down towards his lap, making a loud snap with his fingers! He crinkled up his face, nose and mouth something cute 'n fierce. Then he said:

"Forty years!"

I jumped back too as he continued.

"Forty years I've been waiting for a dream like that! And you? Who are you? Don't even know and you get that dream!"

He then laughed and laughed, so I did too. There then we sat, in bonding laughter, with confirmation of heaven's gift, a sweet little visit by our lovely *Dear Buddha*.

Chapter Three
How little faith I had back then

I needed a yes. My monkey mind was still wild, not wanting to accept the obvious. Little did I know or understand that I was on a journey. I still could not completely accept that I had actually been visited by Buddha. Also, it felt kind of scary.

As a morning dream I had felt total bliss. After sharing with the master masseur and others, I was feeling totally perplexed, thinking there must be some responsibility for me. What was it? I was beginning to match the young man's deep concern. That is when I really began to wonder what was in the files.

During the following week, I received two more powerful dream visions. That is when I was convinced there was a message for me. Maybe even more than one. It was a puzzle.

My conscious spiritual journey began in February 1992. Though I had many answers then in 1999, and knew without a doubt that I was being guided, I was pretty clueless as to understanding what was really going on.

My marriage of 22 years had dissolved. I had been on my own and responsible for two sons since '95. Our eldest was married and a dad himself. I've had the privilege of raising three beautiful sons, a prince each one, a little tiny lord Buddha. Handsome, gorgeous and defiant they are.

These are our children. I ask: if we treat our kids as walking art and all children of God as little tiny golden Buddhas, would we have a more compassionate world?

One week after 9/11, 2001, I had an appointment with a new type of counselor. I needed it. My practical everyday life was still a roller-coaster, emotions going up and down. I had a lot of responsibility and not much in resources. Decision-making was difficult and I thought my children were out of control.

The counselor introduced me to a new concept which felt like home. It was called non-violent communication, introduced by Dr. Marshall Rosenberg.

Little by little this concept gave me a thinking pattern. The philosophy helped pave new steps with security, making the decisions needed on a daily basis, leading me to the life I wanted and to feeling more completion and peace.

I also discovered the healing arts world and began my own healing.

One Day Long Ago

Then one day long ago
I felt
great urgency to write
and said aloud
One day I may.

That day came.
And so I write.
It came one day
last May.

And now a year
obsessed
with inspiration
my tale told.

But hold on,
a new beginning
this is.

27 chapters complete
and now at this
book's end
I write
its beginning.

Sharing my life and woes
I thought
only
a simple tale
needed
only
to find myself

A Guide I need
As *lamplighter*.
And a message
passed on.

Okay!
You tricksters
up there.
Where are you?
Lord, God
of many faces!

What of those files?
Thought of
as Mystery!....
Only now after
17 years, I begin...
to indulge...
in their secrets....

You tricksters!
I say
I had thought it
my story.

Any story
Tall tale
it becomes
as we
witness
ourselves
walking down a path
in Buddha's shoes.

So there you have it, dear *lamplighter*. You may think that you have read the second chapter but it was the last chapter written. Never did I think I'd include this true story of Buddha. I even imagine you read the chapter through.

A need I have to share is, this chapter was not an easy delivery. It took me four weeks to write. I could only write a bit at a time, as if exposing a secret.

The many experiences I have had have been a mystery, even a few 3D miracles and a couple of portal transportations. Truly, I thought these experiences should be private. I have shared some with only a few folks. Now I have processed over the last four weeks the reality of sharing with everyone reading this book. Wow! And okay. Yes, I now write to share.

Here also to speak freely and encourage us all to speak freely about our experiences. And also be willing, to be ready for true miracles!

Out of nowhere, one day I was *inspired* to write. How about that? And so I did. Then for one year I felt an urgency to write 27 detailed chapters. Then one day the urgency I felt, stopped. How's that?

The writings are now divided into three volumes. It was a journey. The journey continued for another year, working with editors and friends. This book is the first volume.

I hope you enjoy the "files" as much as I have and continue to. The chapters (files) prove to be a guide for me, too. A day may go a little rough and so at day's end, I select a chapter to read, to remind myself of who I am. As the guide asks over and over again, who am I? And so it soothes my soul.

Proof to Me

My life is proof
to me
The existence of
Someone
Watching me
Watching you.
You have no idea
What can be
seen
Through the dotted air.
A life unknown.
We, here, now
residing
it clear.
Not.
Who is that

One
Watching me
Watching you.
A woman dear
from a life long past,
Encouraging……..
We, here, now.
have secret
admirers……
Don't even know.
Who are you?
Who am I?
Hoo R U?
Hoo M I?
I M U
U R 2

Who am I? Who are you?

I am a Mystery.
Aren't you too?
Having Mastery Now
A tiny little tad,
You know well what I mean,
Life's many years,

If I am still here,
then some Mastery
   I do have.

Why did I write this?
My dear brother asks,
 This story of Buddha
   What relevance?

I sit now and wonder,
How now? He's the
second kind person, sent
to me I know for sure,
To take time to
   read my manuscript.
Then ask *"Why am I reading this?"*

My quick response is,
 *"I have no idea…
 I was told to write this tale,
 And so I did."*

Now I ask, why?
Again, why me?
Who am I?

*Aha! He says,
cuz I never stop
questioning me.*
Constantly questioned
as a child,

"What's wrong with you?"
Say I now, *"What's right with me?"*

My greatest quest
this life has been
To search
*Who am I? Who are You?
How do we play?*

Who am I? Who are You?

*Is He there? Really?
Watching me, watching you?*

Sharon B said,
*"Well you know how
you've been searching for God all your life…"*
I said *"Noooo…I never knew that. I thought I
was searching for happiness."*

So I pondered…
Contemplating my predicament,
Why did I write?

My brother's voice and glaring eyes,
I then knew he was serious!

Oh dear! Oh my!
What answer?
Buddha now?
I beg thee,
It's so fun…
Let me beg You more,

My soul needs
   baring
My ego has fear,

Tell me Buddha
Why did I write this?
This tale,
tall tale it becomes…
Now… I feel that
Sneaky little smile,
Buddha watching Us!

………..

Happy tears Now.
Beginning to
   Understand
A message.
A heavenly message

I Am brother
I am sister
I am child
I am old
I am senior
I am broken
I am healed
URME
IMU2

Know this:
It takes two to tango,
It takes one to kick
the spurs to
Achilles' destruction.

….

Always remember:
   Love always
   hurt never
Hear thyself

first,
practice words
without spurs,
then Dance.

** ** **

27 chapters
My gift to U.

Martin Wong
   is watching too.
A sweet diagnosed
Schizophrenic,
who once upon a time
   a gift, he was
      too,
This earth he walked
In Buddha shoes.
Full of love
Always love

Sita's first true
teacher of *Art*.
He was *The School*
   of Teaching Art.

Great painter of character scenes.
Compassion he taught
Compassion in his
   heart

Compassion was his Art

Yes, my first teacher,
   consciously

Part II

Chapter Four
What's It All About?

Upon how to write this book I asked myself, how did all this new information rock my world? What was the fundamental gist as to how I found peace? Aha! Fear and anger. Fear and anger are feelings/emotions that have been diminished within me.

When I became a single mother I was terrified. The search for peace and how to get a handle on life was not to be seen easily. I was wild with fear and anxiety.

Little by little I did find tools to guide me on the mental journey I needed to find steps of completion and peace, no matter what was going on. A peace I thought *possible* once I discovered God and angels exist.

Though I was on a quick quest to rid my pain, it's definitely been a turtle race and pace. Here I share, wishing to make a difference.

So What Is It All About?

Dr. Marshall Rosenberg said fear and anger come from <u>a need not met</u>.

Yes, these emotions get encrusted within the walls of our upper belly, the solar plexus of our body.

I was like: *"What's the solar plexus? Isn't it just an energy field?"*

Exactly, and emotions fuel the energy. Feeling pain in the upper belly is proof. Have you ever felt great anxiety in the upper chest, closer to the throat chakra?

So what's really going on? How can I release fear and anger?

Discovering our hidden agendas (HA!) is the key we need!

We have hidden agendas within ourselves which we are not aware of.

These sneaky agendas keep our <u>true needs</u> unmet.

These sneaky agendas lead us on a path to easily justify blame, <u>not understanding all that we are actually *feeling*,</u> and what's really going on. This creates and fuels a generic fear we just live with. It can be subtle.

Then we want more, more in life, more understanding, more love, a deeper love, a better world. More and more we reach to take responsibility for our actions. We know that with honest communication with God and our Higher Consciousness, we do gain a greater sense of authenticity.

We then can be assured we are contributing strongly to a humanitarian world, helping to attain a sense of completion and peace in our life.

Presented here is a way to unlock hidden agendas, help secure self worth and see the bigger picture.

By *Dancing Through Our Light*, that is by walking our talk with compassion, we retain our true nature and our basic need:

the joy of wishing good to all without resentments and qualifications.

Remember the song, *"Be Happy, Don't Worry, Be Happy"?* Hands down, in all my years of various types of counseling, the two most common problems I hear about are: dealing with others and obstacles which seem to be out of our reach. They may create anxiety and great fears of life that keep us in the worry boat. My hope is to unravel this mystery.

Remember the saying *"One day at a time"?* The beautiful point I'd like to make is that we do have *our time.* And it is guaranteed. That is, *we can use our time,* and it is a true reality, guaranteed.

Let us question, what do we do with our time? May we have time, day by day, to create a life with even more love and compassion for ourselves and others? Is it even possible? Absolutely!

Now, as I discover how to write this how-to book, my hope is to take us through a step-by-step process to be happy and feel a life worth its time.

Hey Sam

I've got a plan Sam
to decipher
a map, thought planned out
only to find
more and more obstacles
people's thoughts and actions
to buck me around a bit.
But hold on now!
I've got a new saddle.
This ride should be interesting…

Chapter Five
Let's Check This Out

This guide does refer to God often. Please replace the word God with Higher Consciousness if you prefer, or another endearing term. I grew up with *Papi Dios* and use it once more. It gives me the feeling of true fatherly love. For general deep belief, and a term we all know, here I use God.

Some Pearls of Wisdom

Let us talk about love, something powerful, that is around the world.
We say Love is God. God is Love.
May we then say, God is love in action?

We say His action with us is *loving and has endless mercy*.
May we then say, to mimic God's action is *compassion*?

When we can offer ourselves this kind of compassion,
we take a step toward heaven on earth,
toward happiness.
To actually offer ourselves compassion, takes a good amount of practice.

Dear Lamplighter, let us know that this is *doable*.
An attitude adjustment makes for an easier start, and re-start.

The Big Deal
For attitude adjustment
I'm asking you to Make a Deal with yourself right now,
to continuously
have mercy and be loving toward yourself, always.

"I am, always, loving to myself, and I offer myself mercy when I need it."

Loving means to be understanding,
sweet, honest, caring, protective, wishing well.

Practicing these characteristics paves a conscious compassionate spiritual journey. This practice allows us to explore our God-self, which is the best we can be, motherly and fatherly. Plus, this practice helps us to see the child of God within all others.

Then there is our monkey mind.

The monkey mind is endless. One trick is to give the mind a specific topic to keep it busy. By giving it the topic, *"How to offer compassion,"* the monkey will settle down little by little.

So then, how do we give compassion when anger or fear is thrown at us? Can we do it? Yes!

How do I stop my monkey mind? The scrambling for self-defense upon accusations, or the final intolerance, or wherever else the monkey wants to jump.

A Place of Warmth

To try to mimic God's action <u>is</u> a solution because even the desire to mimic God turns the faucet to warm, a place where anyone, everyone feels warmth.

What Am I Really Thinking? Becoming Aware

It took me two months of **conscious effort to become aware** of what my monkey mind was actually thinking; about myself, about others. The judgments and criticism were constant, big or small; there they were, in my brain. I was truly not aware that my thoughts were so judgmental. I did not use the word, judgmental, more in terms of pro and con. I thought it was normal to navigate through life this way. Becoming *aware* was definitely fundamental in changing my life.

How about you dear lamplighter? What did you grow up with?

Constructive criticism was the norm in my home growing up. Which was totally judgmental. It really never made me feel good about myself. It was not warm.

Therefore I had a deep knowledge that there must be a better way to express myself. I knew that I had a better response and worked best when I was told something positive. Especially if I did not want to do the work being asked of me.

Thoughts constantly floating in my mind had always been there, so why question it? I was a pretty happy person and cared greatly for people. So, I thought I was loving and merciful. Heaven knew I had a good amount of patience and tolerance.

My family had persevered through tremendous conflict. Therefore they thought: by giving 'tear down' criticism then attempting to 'build up' the character by what was their judgment, their opinion of what one did well, was preparing the child/young adult, to handle the outside world. Instead, it broke my confidence. I constantly questioned my self-worth and thought people in general were questioning my ability and thinking process. Therefore, becoming defensive was my norm.

Once I became aware,
I've been able to practice changing a thought when it is lacking compassion.
This helps to turn the faucet to *warm*, especially when talking to myself.
How about that Dear Lamplighter?
It does take practice, practice, and some more practice.
This is where we need patience with ourselves. Awww.

*****

Then, how about when we are talking to another? How do we change the monkey mind?
What do we do with all the criticism?
How do we change a thought when it lacks compassion for another?

Pearl of Wisdom
Connecting is our first step

When we want to mimic God's compassion with another,
first let us <u>acknowledge that we are *connecting, always, every minute.*</u>
Any conversation,
long or short, a passer-by hi and bye,

is a connection, and is a communication.
Any communication is recognized and acknowledged by our soul.
For real!

The joy God gives us is by being loving and merciful, always.
God is understanding, sweet, honest, caring, protective and is always wishing well.

To offer another compassion does not mean we are yielding.
It is the opposite.
We stand grounded with loving self respect,
as we offer a type of respect and love to another.
Compassion is a most powerful action tool we can offer anyone, anytime, anywhere!
Guaranteed!

*****

As we begin to connect with ourselves and all others
in a loving and merciful manner,

we feel deeper connections with more authenticity,
regularly.

As the connection grows,
so does the understanding of the greater picture.

We begin to
understand & feel
God's plan for this complex world
and where we fit in it.

A need begins to grow.
We come to realize the connecting dots and needing to connect even more.

I'd like to share a discovery I made to illustrate this point. This simple story turned on a huge light bulb for me because I had been truly clueless regarding my attitude toward driving, something I did on a regular basis for many years.

Driving

When I had a career which put me on Southern California freeways often, I did not like it. I don't like driving. So, I thought if I hurried it up I could get home sooner. I would drive safely, I thought, leaving space in front just in case. I spent a good amount of time figuring out the positions of the cars to see where and if I could weave through to pass them by and get home sooner.

After a few years, I had discovered a spiritual path and spent time contemplating my new philosophy.

One day, driving as usual, suddenly a fancy car came out of nowhere and was next to me, zooming. Maybe that was its normal. A split second later it was in front of me. Another second or two and it disappeared as it weaved through, safely. My heart jumped because I was about to jump ahead also. If I had, we would have crashed.

My heart thumped with fear. As I watched the car disappear I asked myself, *"How many times did someone's heart jump with fear throughout the years with my safe driving?"* I looked around to see the folks in the cars. They seemed okay. Everyone continued driving.

Then I finally realized, or acknowledged, that I was among a group of people riding in cars on the freeway. We all depended on goodwill and conscious, safe driving from each other. Feeling empathy for each person's perseverance to keep freeway rhythm, I quickly sat back with ease, knowing I could be part of that group.

I then asked myself, "*How can I help make this a nice ride for all of us?*" Quickly I went into offering each person a blessing and thanking them for being cautious, balancing the space between us, offering goodwill to them this day and in their life, asking God to keep us safe and maybe each person feeling a blessing coming their way.

Once I decided to **connect**, I saw/felt each person rather than seeing a car in my way.

I needed to ask myself for forgiveness for having been so blind, so long.

Afterwards, every time I'd drive, I'd have an internal **need to connect** while driving, knowing my role in the big picture. Understanding my goodwill offering was needed for the good vibrations of the entire freeway.

"*Oh maybe she's got a cake in the backseat,*" I'd tell myself when someone was slow or presenting a potential aggravating moment to my limited patience, so as to remind myself that I need to bring my compassion skills to the surface.

As I saw myself as part of the whole group of people in cars on the freeway, I had a need for the whole group to continue driving safely and feeling safe, not just myself. Since we were all driving, the need to get to each destination was in motion. The other need we all had was to feel safe getting there.

I had not been a part of that conscious reality. Realizing the other drivers chose to be in the slower lanes was proof to me that they had this consciousness and I did not. I then and there decided to be a part of that conscious reality. This didn't mean I'd necessarily drive slower. I'd tell myself to drive sweetly with awareness of the other drivers' feelings of safety and ease.

I developed a need to connect.

**This need to connect has truly expanded my heart and world.
It put into action the desire to be part of the solution rather than the problem.**

Bottom line, it is the need to connect compassionately.
Inch by inch this need does transform our world to become humane.
One could say it is the need to connect to the God-force within us.
"*May the Force be with you,*" Yoda ;-)

Dear Lamplighter

Let us develop consciously,
a need to connect,
in a loving and merciful manner with our self, with another.

This is then to mimic God's action, which is
Compassion

This need to connect,
is basic to transforming our world into a loving and merciful planet.

This is truth.
It is indigenous to our soul.

Basic to our nature,
We were born with a need to connect.
From the moment we take our first breath, till the moment we take our last breath, there is:
A need to connect in a loving and merciful manner.

"I am loving to myself and all others, with understanding, sweetness, honesty, caring, protection and wishing well, always. I offer myself and others mercy when needed."

We Pray

*We pray dear Lord
we may expand our world.
Show us your face, your will
gently
as maybe a whisper, a clue
to know how to hear.
Let us need
each other in balanced deed.*

What is it all about then?
It's all about Love.

Chapter Six
NEEDS

There are two points that baffled me regarding the need concept presented by Dr. Rosenberg. First, the idea that we have needs, let alone the idea that I could allow myself to think about them.

I did not grow up poor. But my parents did. Because existence was an issue for them, their needs were sparse. Food and shelter were the only needs I heard of growing up. If I thought of anything else as a need, I thought myself selfish. Never did I recognize having needs. To give was the norm.

The second baffling discovery I had from Dr. Rosenberg's list of universal needs was a "need to celebrate" one's life.

Really? I thought except for food and shelter anything else was a want.

Birthday parties were for somebody else. My mother feared that too much fuss could create a haughty, loud, demanding adult. Birthdays were not celebrated in her village. It was not something she missed out on. I accepted her truth and was taught to give even more to prove my self-worth. As in worthy of *being* or existing.

My mom did not realize I missed out on anything or how unworthy I felt. She did not realize how it contributed to the segregation I found at school. As a result, I thought I should not have a **need** to be included and tried to negate my feelings of sadness and loneliness by adopting her truth.

So, how about that? We all have needs. All of us.

There are universal needs like safety and celebrating. Then there are all kinds of needs throughout the day, all day long. Needs like going to work, or grocery shopping, staying on schedule, etc. These are **personal needs.**

And how about a need ….
To feel comfortable in a conversation with another.
To feel safe in order to state one's truth.

And how about a need to feel uplifted, courageous, valued, happy, content, satisfied?
These are real personal needs too.
These needs are feelings, that exist within us. We are capable of bringing them to the surface.

Here's a little loving homework.

We need feelings.
Feelings are emotions within us. With practice, feelings can surface.

Ask yourself to feel love now.
Take a couple of seconds to fill yourself.
If it is difficult, remember a time you felt love…

****

Love draws in your highest good.
Love drives you to your right path.

To practice sitting in love, sit inside a circle of love.
Expand yourself within your highest good.

As *lamplighters, the need*
to love, to seek love, and to be love
is a number-one need in our life.

****

Let us differentiate between need and needy.

To even use the word 'need' so much in acquiring the skills of compassionate language felt uncomfortable to me. After all, I didn't like the idea of being needy. Then I remembered Barbara DeAngelis' cute story on this subject.

In a seminar, a young man stood up and said he didn't like the 'need'. It made him feel needy. Barbara asked if he was in a relationship. He said no. She asked if he wanted one. Yes, he replied. She then asked the audience if anyone wanted to use the restroom facilities. A few hands went up. Then she asked if anyone *needed* to use the restroom facilities. No hands. She turned and answered the young man. There were no hands raised because if anyone needed the facilities they would not be sitting here in the audience, they'd be in the restroom. Needs push us to do, to take action.

Needs are within us, and they make us take action. How about that?

Anything and everything we do, any action and reaction we have,
is the result of fulfilling a need.
For real!

May I repeat this, please?

Needs are within us, and they make us take action.
Anything and everything we do, any action and reaction we have,
is the result of fulfilling a need.
For real!

Then:
our needs stimulate our emotions
and the reverse:
our emotions stimulate our needs.

****

The Need is the Key We Need
to unlock hidden agendas (Ha!)

We then come to understand,
the motivation
behind our action.

We go from Ha! to, Aha!
Let us find that Key!

Look at it like a new crossword puzzle;
feeling, crossing with the need; **need** crossing with motivation.

We ask ourselves: *What am I actually thinking? What **need** has not been met?*
"Why did I do that?
"Why did I say that?
"Why do I feel this?
What **need** has not been met?
Or, *what need do I think I need?* Therefore, the need pushed me to do something unwanted or that has ill consequences?"

A simple example: I miss a right turn and now with traffic I may be late for my appointment.

I begin to tense up, so I ask myself,

"Why did I miss the turn, what need pushed me to do that?"

Quickly I realized **my need** to know what to say to my client, overran my present focus on driving, thus I missed the turn. Rather than becoming upset with myself, I begin to process my actions with *passion for compassion.* This is exactly how we begin to give ourselves love and empathy.

Then I continue to talk to my inner self with the dialog of being loving and merciful to me by asking, *what am I thinking, what am I feeling?* This is being motherly and fatherly.

"Aha! I feel tension because I have fear of being late." Okay, what need do I have that makes me want to be on time?

The obvious answer is to be efficient. What is the need behind that? What is my hidden agenda?

Aha! The need to make a good impression. I need to show that I care. This is also my personal, bottom-line need.

> *It is a hidden agenda because it was not obvious.*
> *To find the hidden agenda, pro or con, is a jewel!*
> *Like a crystal gem!*

Now that I know my personal need, that is to make a good impression and show I care, I know what I can do. The inner dialog continues,

"I know that if I'm late, I can still fulfill my bottom-line personal need by offering the assurance that I care. This I know I can do."

My next **need is**: how to drop the tension? With the acknowledgement of knowing that I can offer assurance, I can quickly answer this question,

"So what can I do to make myself feel better right now? How may I drop the tension? Aha! Surface confidence."

The feeling of confidence had been diminished as fear took me over with the thought of being late.

The tension now drops.

This is an example of a simple problem that can be quickly processed with practice. A more complicated situation benefits from the same process, and may require more time.

> Figuring out my need,
> allowed me to understand myself with more completeness and see my bigger picture.

Rather than to stay in fear with the thought, "*I must get there on time*" and become nervous with the thought of my client's potential anger for having to wait, I retain my self worth.

By bringing confidence to the surface, I easily feel confident. Why? Because I understand that my main **need** is to give my client assurance that I care. This is something that I know I can do.

Fear and anger keep us from "seeing" our full picture, our complete potential, diminishing our self-worth, diminishing our personal needs, keeping us in the 'worry boat', creating some blame and shame.

Confidence is a strong emotion -- we need to do what we need to do. It is also an easily recognizable emotion. And it is an emotion we want to retain.

Pearl of Wisdom: Personal Needs gives us Confidence

If I am lacking confidence at any point, I ask *"Why? What do I need, what is missing, why did my confidence diminish? There is the obvious circumstance. Is something more? What is it that broke my sense of strong will?"*

Then I ask myself, *"What am I needing?"* This is a wonderful question! Why?

For example, in the above story, figuring out the need showed me the bigger picture of my own life! That of acknowledging the need to make a good impression and the need to show I care. These are **personal needs that I can fulfill.** This is why we use the term - personal needs. The needs are something inside of me that I can do for myself.

This way I do not, cannot, focus on fears nor allow my client to shame me in any manner. Why? Because my attention is now centered on what can be accomplished: reassurance and confidence. This processing retains my confidence and self-worth with a gentle pride. Awww.

Most people, if given the chance, want to naturally focus on the positive.

If my client likes to stress efficiency, and I am late, because I stayed focused on confidence and goodwill, chances are the client will feel the vibrancy of reassurance and caring. I then can seal the deal because I can draw the client to focus on what is most important to her/him, and to me: feeling assured.

Should my client continue to stress on efficiency after a sincere apology and offering reassurance, then I would need to make a decision, yes or no, to work with that type of focus which would be stressful. Yes or no.

Soul Connection is the Expansion We are Looking For

The idea to search for the **need** that motivates another person's action, takes us to a deeper understanding, allowing us to *hear* more, to be more present and comprehend their bigger picture.

This is a big deal.
This is Soul Connection.
It is also called *empathy*. We listen and wait….. Wait to hear more.
We can help paint the picture to be uplifting.
With our passion for compassion we encourage sacredness to our lives. Aww.

With expanding our hearts and minds for a powerful world healing,
we can help to paint a new picture.

Should I continue to work with a client or someone who works with stress, as in the above example, then I know as *lamplighter*, some of the challenge I will be accepting. This is also a big deal! Why? The search for how to connect soul to soul and hear a deeper truth may be the expansion we all need for a healing yet to be seen.

As *lamplighters*,
we know we hold the responsibility with loving care,
determining how long we can/need to work with this client,
holding the blue flame of empathy for ourselves and the client.

****

Another example, when some gossip begins to rise up in a conversation, ask yourself, *"What need is there behind these words? How can I hear the deeper story?"*

Little by little you may ask a question or two, to help decipher what's really important, what need we should talk about, what's really going on.

Conversation can be great fun, entertaining and uplifting, helpful and insightful.

By asking pertinent questions, one may turn the gossip into a personal group adventure of self discovery, affirmation, validation and hope for the future.

To me, people, including myself, love to talk about ourselves. Why? Not because of self flattery but actually to feel support, camaraderie and compatibility, to feel connected and have a sense of solving world problems. :-)

Gossip also includes our own monkey mind when alone.
One evening as I was editing this manuscript, I realized I had been going over a couple of situations that I thought I had no control over and was complaining to myself. Gossip.

As I read the above 'gossip guide', I realized I could ask myself, *"Where am I going with this complaining?*
What adventure am I seeking out?
An adventure to make me feel bad that I need to deal with some difficult situations?
No, I don't want that! I am needing affirmation and validation.
No, I do not need flattery.
I need to feel supported and connected. Where or how do I get that?"

Immediately I realized I was gossiping to myself. And I could stop it now by focusing on my personal <u>real bottom-line need,</u> and ask what is within my capacity to fulfill my needs?

With this realization and question, I could feel the frustration float away. I then began the adventure of expansion and freedom. I could then begin to answer, "How may I enhance my life?"

Yes, by delving into our personal needs, we search for that which may enrich our lives.

****

Daily Menu

To ask ourselves these questions, daily, helps the mind to learn a new process.
That which will enrich all of our lives. Guaranteed!

What are my needs? What am I thinking?
What are my bottom-line needs? Personal needs?
What is it that I can do? A need that I can do for myself?
How may I enhance my life, and it be for the greater good?

Dear Lord

Oh Dear Lord
a need we have
You alone know
what motivated us.
Your Will
My Will
as this life unfolds
why did I come?
Dear Lord
to know my need
fully
to understand
that drive...
What motivates me?
Why am I here?

Allow it
to unfold
my friend...

My quest
My thirst
to know
How do we roll?

My needs are
universal
that I do know

What creature
here on earth
can hear presently?
or shall I say
What here
on earth presently
is prepared to
hear this creature's
sound?

Chapter Seven
Connecting

As we lamplighters continue on our journey, we become aware of our intuition. We realize the sense of something, the hunch we had that came true, a powerful dream, a coincidence, happening over and over. We are connecting.

Similar to a cell phone, we are sending messages to each other through our continuous connection. The difference is we have had a connection going on for thousands of years. Or forever. This truth intrigues me.

Experiencing this truth, becoming aware and actually feeling connections is what convinced me of God's existence and that some sort of heavenly order is at hand. This is how I sealed the deal with myself that God exists.

As an atheist, I could not accept the happenings. I did not understand them. I feared them. They were beginning to prove me wrong. Overwhelmed with realizing the reality of the happenings, I began to record them, simply writing them down as some sort of proof that they had occurred. I was determined to figure out what was true.

After about three years, I was recording my happenings early one morning when, suddenly I felt a nice feeling surge within me. I sat back wondering what I was feeling. Little by little I began to feel bliss! As the bliss grew within me and then to all parts of me, I somehow felt an explosive outward connection to all people around the world. I did not cry, I did not laugh. I did feel the largest smile across my face, my cheeks almost aching with the force of the grin. I was ecstatic!

The fear then vanished. It was replaced with the knowing that somehow God is and I could connect with Him and anyone.

My life continued and so did the happenings. I did not fight them any longer, as if I could, anyway. It had been a struggle within.

Finally I was convinced that a heavenly order or heavenly organization is orchestrating our awareness of connecting. This awareness of a heavenly order orchestrating connections has expanded my world!

It is like a *3-D God web*, a type of three dimensional netting which is being connected every second! Aha! As in: we are human beings, who are *being* in the state of connection every second, whether we recognize it or not.

Once I realized a 3-D connecting web exists, my logical Capricorn mind then told me that somewhere there is a solution to any dilemma or problem I may ever have. All I need to do is ask for the connection to lead me to the solution and simply wait to be hooked up.

How about that? And it has worked without fail, always.

At times the solution has not been my desire, my hope. That's where the feeling comes in.

**Truly feeling the connection to the bigger picture
gives us a deep understanding to accept what is best for all,
to accept God's plan,
to accept, life's purpose,
and how we fit in it...**

When the connection can be felt, with acceptance kicking in, is when one may sacrifice at will. This has happened throughout history in many heroic feats in war and protection. The soldier feels his companions are in danger and instantly receives an inspiration to action in order to save his buddies, sacrificing his own life.

A mom feels her child is in danger, and instantly receives an inspiration. She then knows what action to take. It doesn't matter if she needs to sacrifice herself to any degree.

We do accept God's will more often than we realize.

By sitting with God, asking for a direct connection to feel His presence, fills my being with love. From there I can wait with ease to be hooked up to the connection I need to find my solution. It may be through an inspiration, my intuition, or the solution may be through a person. It may be through a series of events or through a series of events with people's help.

**This is the way connection works, whether we have awareness or not.
This realization was even greater proof of God's existence,
of a profound heavenly order.**

Through this awareness, I have been able to develop my intuition, consciously. First, by asking, then waiting to feel filled with God's love. Next, **get ready to receive information** regarding what is needed now, plus awareness of my guided path going forward.

If going forward takes a long time and my drama queen wants to surface with her monkey mind, then I need to go through the loving procedure again, beginning with asking. Sometimes the second step of waiting to be filled with God's love is as far as I can go. Receiving knowledge or a feeling for the solution is not at hand, yet.

Sometimes the "not at hand, yet" seems like a sacrifice because it can be gut wrenching, actual pain. It is because at that point we are feeling the connection. The closer the connection -- to a loved one, a comrade or in having great sympathy for a person or situation -- can definitely cause actual bodily pain.

When this happens it is hard to feel filled with God's love, even though I know the love *is*. This is why I thrive in the art of compassionate language.

How I speak to myself
can work with my heart and feelings to help heal
my soul and cure my bodily pain.

This is accomplished by becoming aware.
Aware of what I am actually thinking, feeling and needing;
to connect with my soul.

Real Connections, Beyond Our Wildest Dreams

This is a lovely story, dear lamplighter. Soon after my mother crossed over to and beyond the Pearly Gates of Heaven I received an unexpected visit. She might have been part of the Heavenly Conspiracy to make the sweet connection.

Mama Lupe did not grow up with a local church in her tiny tiny Mexican village, *Lluvia de Oro, Rain of Gold*. However the folks still had great faith and welcomed the spirit world. She therefore did not have an attachment to the church, until her son died. I was born a year later and was raised on their lovely Hacienda Ranch in the USA.

Mama felt a burden with the death of her son and developed a strong attachment to the church. It was too much for me as she tried to make me, too, have a strong attachment. When I was grown she was well aware of my atheistic values. She pleaded with me and prayed that I'd come back to God.

Well, she won! She prayed with her strong faith that would someday bring me back. The first miracle I had with her was when I was 27. I had been in a car accident when I was 20 and suffered a whiplash injury, always needing a scarf as my neck was continuously cold and had some pain.

Mama Lupe had gone on a Holy Land tour and brought back some holy water from Lourdes. She asked if she could massage some on my sore neck and I said okay. But then she began to pray and asked if I believed. I answered that I couldn't lie and said no I don't believe.

Well, wouldn't you know it, the next day the pain was gone! After 7 long years! I figured that because her faith was so strong, somehow she was able to put some kind of something on me and let it go at that. I wasn't about to allow myself to question it further.

About 20 years later I did become a God devotee once more. Mama Lupe passed away a few years later.

I loved her love for her dining room set. She had great pride and joy in seating her guests, often a dinner for 12. I thought the table held such grand stories and felt appreciative ….. and somehow I also felt totally enchanted to receive her dining room table and chairs.

The table could fold down to seat only six, she liked to explain. So then, after a couple of decades, Mama had such delight to get an extension so that the table could seat up to 20!

Taking the set home helped to lift my sadness that she was gone.

Gone with her was also an era of time. An era of the late 1800's, continuing into the early 20th century. She was the youngest of her siblings and the last to go. Mama was born in 1911. My papa and his siblings had already been gone for twelve long years.

Little by little, I began to get uplifted. Then considering that I was born in 1950 and that it was now the year 2000, I realized a totally new era was being launched in our huge extended family! I felt honored as I set up the family table in my home.

Taking my time to arrange the table and chairs, I was simply mesmerised by the memory of her passionate joy in doing the same. Then, too, I became very joyful! I felt happiness and was truly inspired! I also felt very calm.

It was late at night by the time I finished. Feeling satisfied with the arrangement, I stepped back to get a better view and said out loud in a whisper:

"Well here you have it. Don't know exactly where you all go. Or where you all have gone. But I know you are all gone from us now. I've set up Mama's table here now in my home and I invite you. Anyone who wants a home to come and visit, here it is."

Goodness knows, I could not have imagined back then that someone could actually be hearing me! What a surprise! Though I did believe in an afterlife, not understanding it at all, I was still in the mood of playing and pretending!

As I walked down stairs the next morning and turned the corner, I could easily see a whole bunch of ghosts like beings sitting around the table! Do you think I was hallucinating? Shock does not even begin to describe the ginormous expansion going through my mind! It was like everything I knew was instantly erased!

Thinking of myself as a totally mature person and priding myself with being logical, the connection I was witnessing was breaking all logical barriers! It was a connection of heaven touching earth! The connection of life touching death! The witnessing of another form after what we call death!
And they were having a party! All around the table!

I ran down the rest of the stairs. They were simply sitting there, watching me run down the stairs. And they were smiling! All 12 of them, sitting around the table. Smiling!

I thought it was like a cartoon. But it was real! They were somewhat transparent but in full view. Then magically the whole table top was filled with smaller ghosts or maybe more transparent, like one on top of the other or maybe like a bouquet.

As I approached the table, they all vanished but I could still feel them. I was a little disappointed but my excitement with acknowledging this reality was beyond any other emotion. I was ecstatic! The connection I was continuing to feel was powerful and most enjoyable. Feeling the connection is what really sealed the deal with me that what I had witnessed was real! I could feel them strongly for a while! My mind was quiet. Even the air felt different, for a while.

****

Since then I have believed that miracles are available to us.
They are available through our connections.

*There are Celestial warm beings out there, somewhere, connecting and helping us 24/7
* They'd like to be connected with us consciously.
How about that?
*We really can connect with anyone, consciously.
Simply by asking.
Asking and inviting
in total ceremony,
that is, with
reverence, honor and respect.
Aww.

Thank You Dear Lord

Sending messages
And inspiration for our lives.
We pray for guidance
To recognize an opportunity
To connect consciously,
Appreciating You gracing us
With your bonding connecting dots

Chapter Eight
Feelings

Feelings and Needs are within us always, 24/7. We do use our mind to discern our needs yet it is our feelings that will enable us to take action. Acknowledging our feelings is basic to our being. We might have been taught otherwise. Let us check this out, Dear Lamplighter. This chapter offers a shift in acknowledging who we are and how-to communicate with our deepest self.

A Lamplighter's Guide to Soul Communication
The gateway to communicating with our soul is by acknowledging what we are feeling.
We then talk to our deepest self.

Let's start at the beginning, our birth.

Gratitude. Gratitude is a feeling, a natural, honest and sincere emotion that we actually can and do easily feel. Gratitude is one of our very first, and basic feelings.

What happens soon after birth? We have a need to eat and nurse. *This need* produces so much pain, a strong feeling of hunger, that the need becomes the main focus.

When we are able to nurse and our tummy fills with milk there is an insurmountable amount of gratitude. By receiving nourishment and feeling gratitude, happiness surfaces. Someone may remark the baby is drunk on Mommy's milk and is in pure bliss! Awww.

Gratitude is a natural feeling which is recognized and differentiated then, soon after birth. It does not matter that a baby has no verbal vocabulary or a thinking mind able to rationalize the sequence of events which led to happiness. The baby felt discomfort, and then felt gratitude, then felt happiness.

As infants, we automatically feel a feeling. Maybe the differentiating of feelings came even before birth? Without doubt, differentiating feelings is something natural to all of us.

As we grow, we develop a vocabulary. We use our mind to do this. Rationalization also begins its journey. First we begin to recognize sequences. When I cry I get to nurse, my tummy feels full and the hunger pain disappears. Pretty simple.

Soon we actually rationalize crying to express a feeling: pain. We hope for the sequence that leads to happiness. There is no verbal vocabulary, just an understanding of a rationalization. A baby easily figures out the sequence, then somehow rationalizes, *"Aha! If I cry, I get to eat!"*

Imagine other feelings that develop, or that are recognized at a very early age.
How would a person develop if he/she were introduced to great amounts of fear at an early age?
How about being raised with a minimal amount of fear?
What about tension between adults? Does the infant feel/recognize one adult from another along with the emotions the person is carrying?

We know without a doubt that a baby can feel love and prefers it. Yes!

As a baby therefore,
we maneuver around and about with awareness of our environment through what we are feeling.
How about that?

So basically, we are what we feel.

****

**How, then, does rationalizing come about?
And how do we use it?**

Pearls of Wisdom
Only as an infant and as a child, we have our normal needs
plus
we have an added need to be totally dependent.
Pretty simple, yes?

Because we are dependent on caregivers
as a growing infant,
our mind tries to put feelings (something we are born with)
and
the understanding of interactions with caregivers (something experienced)
into some sort of order.
We begin then,
the process of rationalizing our actions to get our normal needs met.
"Aha! If I cry I get to eat!"

This means that
as a child, in order to have some equilibrium
and get our natural needs met,
the mind will eventually begin to shut down some feelings,
and
it will begin to scramble
a rationalized story with individual emotions.
This is a big deal!

Whenever any of our basic needs are a struggle,
our rationalizing with scrambling thoughts and feelings is increased.

When we rationalize, we want it to be for the highest good.
We can change our thinking process for the highest good through compassion.
Help us Dear Lord to understand

****

Let us continue these Pearls of Wisdom

It is easy and normal to not understand what we are really thinking and feeling.
We soon develop mixed up priorities because of the values in our environment,
such as fear and anger,
greed and control.
Priorities: that fear, anger, greed and control run our life.
Oh Dear! Oh My! Holy Moly!

This is not our nature.
We were taught to separate our persona from our soul and call it our ego,
something to be feared. How about that?

These are all the makings of hidden agendas. Ha!
For example: like the ego that takes us over, without control.
Naturally this would be feared.

Let us expand ourselves to the highest good.
and become friends with our ego.
This is the next step.

****

Prioritizing that we are what we feel,
our soul and persona (ego) are in tune.

This automatically teaches a youngster
that one cannot make another person into something.
Everyone's choices and destiny can only be controlled by the self.

Why?
We would know that each person has a different method of gauging success and happiness. From our birth we would be raised with this higher frequency, that of allowing each person to be.

If we truly want to serve our higher self and a humanitarian world, we want to be able to get beyond our own self doubts and illusions, which cause shame and guilt, taking time away from achieving all that we can.

We can do more, be more,
always motivated by the strongest and bravest feeling in existence,
love.

By unraveling our thinking process, we come to understand even more that we are not this body.

We are a soul that has come to earth, which experiences a life on earth. We were driven here by our emotions' from our last life, bringing to this life whatever emotions were not fulfilled. This is our truth.

Dear Lamplighter,
This is a journey as to how to listen to our soul and persona/personality/ego. The strongest connection to a tangible conversation between our soul and our ego, therefore, is our feelings. How about that? We use our mind as a tool to do this; to have the conversation. What am I feeling? What do I need?

Feelings and Needs are within us always, 24/7.
We do use our mind to discern our needs
yet it is our feelings that will enable us to take action.

Our primary and basic, personal need is
to be free in mind and spirit; to be in the space of offering
loving goodwill to all, naturally.
Our feelings of joy and feeling connected are our soul's journey.

****

This next story had me perplexed for many years. It was an emotional occasion that made no sense to me. That is, I had no understanding of how or why my ego had such an outburst. Only now, through this lamplighter's guide, have I been able to understand it more.

Expressions and Explosive Tears

When I was a young adult, I saw that I was a crybaby at times. It bothered me. Finally I realized my crying was a curse and my forte. The connections I felt, though unaware, pushed me to tears. They also gave me great relief and the release of bottled up emotions which only sometimes was I able to express in words.

One day I was conversing with two young men when it became somewhat heavy. Feeling my eyes begin to fill with water, I felt fear in my heart with a bit of anger wanting to surface in my solar plexus, upper belly. Determined to voice my will and not allow myself to feel cowardly, I simply blurted out, *"I may begin to cry, I'm emotional and I need to continue talking."*

To my surprise, the two men were completely capable of accepting my crying while hearing the information I needed to voice. It also did not seem to hinder an honest response. If anything, what I remember is that we were able to get to the understanding we needed from each other, finding solutions and having a sense of completion with smiles.

I was shocked with myself for blurting out with words and tears to total strangers. I also felt an extra weakness because I thought that I was outnumbered, that I would get minimized and be considered an out-of-control pathetic female. Our conversation had no financial impact for any of us. That I do remember.

So why did I go there? Why did I allow myself to cry? Why didn't I change the subject, walk away or do something other than cry?

Recently I had processed my 'curse,' asking myself, *"Why do I just start crying at different times, what is wrong with me?"* It made me think I was sick or stupid. At the time I had no solution other than I could easily feel my feelings which led me to have more authenticity and overall happiness. Therefore I decided I could accept my curse.

As I was beginning to feel overwhelmed by the conversation, I knew if I bottled up my truth, I would not be happy with myself. My need to voice my truth was all consuming, and was the only thing I could focus on. The crying was an interference and an extreme emotional expression that I did not want, so I found the need to explain myself. "I'm a crybaby, so I may cry, but don't pay attention, I just need to talk."

Looking back I can say by crying, and by stating my need to speak anyway, I was offering my vulnerability, my common humanness, my deep inner self, without any blame or accusations.

Also I confirmed and assured them that my crying had nothing to do with my listeners. I believe they felt confidence, sensing no accusations. Therefore a door was quickly opened to our humanness and to our truth. Then, they also had the need to express a deeper self. Because we went there, expressing a deeper self, a better sense of connecting came in, giving us all a greater sense of completion, leaving us to look deeply into each other's eyes for a second, creating a loving bond expressed in huge smiles and dancing eyes.

In this story, I had a personal need to voice my truth. Because my feelings were pushing me to tears, I had to explain myself or defend/excuse myself and assure my listeners they were not at fault. I did not know how to express my feelings. Because I felt them strongly, my physical self had no outlet but to cry. Actually, feeling them strongly produced tears of anger. I did not want to feel anger so I exploded with tears.

Today, because I have practiced the art of passion for compassion, I rarely have the need for explosive angry tears.

I have continuous joy, knowing I can express my needs and feelings, safely, anywhere, at any time. It is a struggle at times, but I know I have it within me to figure it out, compassionately.

How about that?

****

By offering vulnerability,
that is by offering how we feel and a personal need,
without accusations, demands, criticism, expectations, guilt-- am I forgetting anything?
We offer our humanness.
Our common humanness and our deepest self.

This may open a door for another to express their humanness,
their inner truth and their feelings.
Why?
Because each of us has a…

Need to connect in a loving and merciful manner.
It is natural.
It is indigenous.
We may trust this.
We can bank on it.
Yes, we can take this truth and put it in the bank!
Guaranteed to be a most valued treasure!
We have a need to connect.

A Passion for Compassion

P.S. Shortly after writing this chapter, one day I awoke remembering the actual story. I met with these two young men to talk about a possible real estate sale. Quickly we realized the financial project was not to be, but continued talking about the area.

I had thought the conversation was about an underdog, which usually brings out my emotional bag of feelings. Well, it was.

We were all new to the area, figuring out how to get established. We were in our twenties. We also had similar skin and hair color. People do not recognize me as being Mexican.

Eventually the conversation was not fun for me. I could not allow these two folks to continue believing what they were saying and thinking about Mexicans.

Naturally they were surprised to hear that I was of Mexican descent. Often even Mexicans get surprised.

As I was "nicely" trying to set them straight, I began to fill with emotional tears because I was so angry and did not want to start yelling. Foremost I wanted to be nonviolent. But the dragon in me had been fueled and I needed a release. My physical chemistry changed into the form of explosive tears.

Knowing back, even then, that we are all one, as in one people, I knew if I talked about the struggle my family had to give me the freedom I now live, just like all Americans with a foreign lineage, and explain, as gently as I could, with all the love of my being, I would be heard and my tears possibly understood.

I knew this truth could not be denied and the two would remember meeting a Mexican on their terms.

My greater truth, my personal need, was a need to express my views which I knew were opposing theirs. I did not want them to have their views! That's the part in me that triggered a bag of emotions!

I wanted them to have different views. But .... the greater anger came from me thinking that I could demand that they have different views. I began to judge them as inhumane and wrong. Basically, my ego wanted control! This is something that I was taught. That I could try to demand it in one way or the other. How about that? That I could control through anger or through tears (the victim).

It has taken me decades to fully understand this anger. I didn't know about expressing my bottom-line personal need, which was for *me* to work towards a humanitarian world. I didn't think of expressing that their views were contrary to mine and the difference was stirring my feelings of fear and anger because I wanted to like them! Could it have been that simple? It takes a vulnerability to go there.

This type of honesty can make us feel vulnerable. How about that?

Like most of us, I was taught and trained that my focus should stay on something right or wrong and on accountability. Rather than on my real self and the need for connection.

But really my focus stayed on something that was out of my control! So my ego exploded with anger! How about that? Angry tears.

Releasing the many different layers of anger
gives us an expansion towards freedom like no other.

It hasn't been simple and easy to express our true selves, dear lamplighter. We were taught otherwise. With practice we do develop a new norm. Guaranteed. I invite you now to a whole new world. Somewhere safe and loving, always. Where we share our real self and create deeper connections and relationships. Awww.

In this story, because I already wanted non-violence as a priority in my life, I had a hunch that my vulnerability and heart would open their hearts. And it did. The two strangers, finally not so strange any longer, immediately began to own up to the facts of their own grandparents' struggle. They showed me that they, too, had a connection to know, understand and feel the possible pain I was trying to express. They also were sharing the grand fact of being connected through our mutual stories and our feelings. Oh, so sweet.

*So there we stood, for one second or two, I remember well, looking deeply into each other's eyes,
knowing
our lives were now changed because we met.*

How about that?

Can we ever know?

With whom to connect?
To share our ever
evolving self

A stranger, a friend
Should the time arise
May I arise
Step Up to

the occasion in life
with its mysteries?

Never know
What's lurking yonder
A conversation
A connection

with one who
Too
Is gracing this Earth.

With knowledge
Shared
A word
A laugh
A tear
A story

This life
We live
We must
We can
Muster up

A team
Inside of me
A universe
of possibilities

Chapter Nine
Spiritual Needs

Dear Lamplighters, as we become more aware of our spiritual journey we develop spiritual needs. What are spiritual needs?

When I thought I was an atheist and threw away the concept of God, I needed a replacement. I questioned why we had developed a God. I actually inquired as to the need humans had to dream up the concept of God.

Here is what I came up with.

However we developed, whatever theory we want to adopt, God, evolution, UFO, it can't be denied that we are here. We are also a natural being, a critter, a standing and walking creature who is born naturally and who dies naturally.

We also have detailed interactions with other beings. The details become all time consuming so we become detached from our natural state.

After a period of detachment, the being in us, begins to have a great need to commune with nature. A sense of merging with that which is natural, like we are.

It is a natural need.

Being a dancer, I also had a feel for the air with movements going through it. Air is also natural. I had a hunch there was something to do with movement or expression and nature and the need for God.

A Little Movie

Suddenly I received an inspiration. It was in the form of two short film clips.

The first was a surfer riding a wave. Then he was sitting on the surfboard floating over calm waters. His happy face was raised to the soft sunshine. He was feeling bliss, in tune with nature, feeling complete.

The second was a priest at the altar, preparing Holy Communion for his congregation. He had prepared by cloaking himself in the proper robes. He was offering reverence for his faith and felt humbled and satisfied. He also felt honored to be selected by the Lord to bless the congregation, feeling appreciation. He waved his arms in selected directions. Then knelt down for a second. He felt bliss, complete, and in tune with something which has always been, God.

It was then that I began to feel satisfaction, realizing we all wanted the same thing.

It is the need to be in tune.
In tune with nature.
In tune with something that has always been.

With this little vision, I was led to think that to get in tune, we need to do something with our physical, natural self, and connect with nature in its purity. The surfer and the priest were at the same point in satisfying a need for God, to connect with something that has always been. This insight gave me great satisfaction in my search to replace the void I felt when I became an atheist.

The other thing I saw was the authenticity in their intentions and sincerity in their actions to attain the connection.

As an atheist, authenticity and sincerity were a growing need in my life. Little by little I was developing these virtues as personal values to live by. Therefore, this vision somehow gave me further satisfaction to justify my atheistic philosophy. It carried me through another decade of being a self-proclaimed atheist. The funny part of this story is that I never questioned how in the world I could get a vision or even an inspiration? Aha! and Haha!

Now I do believe in God, a higher power, one to whom I may talk and ask for assistance.
One who is loving and merciful and has always been.

****

Becoming Aware of Personal Spiritual Needs

People sometimes say to me they feel so much better when they are on their spiritual path, but that they haven't had the time to dedicate to it.

We know we are all on a spiritual journey. Truly, death can happen at any time. So, really, we have our priorities when it comes to time.

When someone says they feel better when they're on their spiritual path, I believe they are talking about needing rituals. Rituals give us a sense of being sacred. What is a ritual? The priest had his and so did the surfer.

Our need to commune with nature/God may be expressed through our natural 'critterness.'
That is, physically touching nature somehow,

with reverence and honor,
having great intention for authenticity, sincerity, and gratitude!

Dance became my ritual.

Singing joyful noise to the Lord is a ritual.
It doesn't matter if it's in tune, as long as our heart is in tune.

Lighting a candle and saying a prayer.

Picking or buying flowers, and arranging them on the dinner table with love,
honor and reverence for family or friends can be a ritual.

Blessing our food and water
with hands in sacred motion, or holding connecting hands in
reverence and honor for God the Creator, the gardener and food distributor.

We lamplighters have a need for spiritual ritual.
Developing a ritual, a way to commune with God, offers us a way to
communicate with God, consciously.
Yahoo! ;-)
The more we practice, the quicker we feel a merging with God.
Communication grows.

****

Here are some of my favorite rituals.

*At birthday time, a picture of the birthday girl or boy is placed on the house altar with great reverence. Sending prayers, offering flowers.

*Upon waking in the morning, I look out the window to capture and honor God's first light, giving thanks.

*My day starts with saying good morning to God. Checking in with myself to see how I feel in case I have a need for a conversation with God. Over time I have been drawn to give more and more time to communing with God in the early morning. The dawn of day has grown to have more meaning for me. Now I need at least a couple of hours. Should circumstances require my time, then 5 to 10 minutes is a good go for me. Every day.

*When I step outside, I must greet all my plant friends. I tell them how beautiful they are, how grateful I am to share my life with them, grateful they are here. I tell God what a great Creator He is. I thank Him for letting me be here and I thank Him for protecting us. Every day.

*When I buy gifts or receive gifts, including paychecks and weekly food, I place them on the family altar for a while, offering my bounty to our dear sweet Lord, asking for blessings. I ask for blessings for the person who gifted me and whom I may be gifting.

I ask to be guided as to how to spend the money received, wisely. When the gifts are in cash, I ask that the energy held be purified and guided to continue doing good for all.

Then, thanking our dear Lord for the scrumptious veggies and food, I ask for even more blessings, with the desire to pass those blessings on.

*****

There is one ritual I am beginning to set in motion and hope many will join in.
*Water blessings.
   Created in ceremony with reverence and honor.
   Alone or with a group of friends, create a sacred space.
   Invite God, angels, saints and loved ones who have passed on to the pearly gates of heaven.

Have a pitcher of fresh water ready to bless.
   Create a circle.
   Pass the water to each person.
   Each person gives it a private blessing while the rest are in silent prayer.
   Then pass it on to the next.
When the circle is complete, offer group prayers and maybe singing.
   Plus any other ideas you may develop, to bring in even more, extra love.
When the ceremony is complete, fill little spray bottles and share.
This is a wonderful ritual to help shift energy in homes and workplaces.
Offer room blessings for a sick friend. This ritual is limitless. And it is powerful!
Honored with the grace of God, continuously.

The Art of creating a ritual is limitless.

To be in tune with that which has always been.
We beings like to create and enjoy
daily rituals.
With purest intentions,
we offer reverence and honor to our lives. Awww.

Open the Window

Open the window dear Lord
May I smell
Your fresh air
With fragrance
Radiating
in your smile.

May I lift my head
To absorb more
The heavenly spray
of a fragrance
Known
Jasmine, rose and
Sweet gardenias
known to float
on bathing waters
Here on earth
To wash our sorrows

Golden heavenly fragrance

To lift
My spirit.

I find that radiance
so soft and
Subtle.

Sweeping me
My wholeness
Seeking Thee
Today
Tomorrow,
I live now
knowing
My spirit
Rides,
Needing
Recognition
No doubt!

No Doubt

I sing my sorrows
For they hold me
down, not
As I come to need,

To recognize
No doubt!

My need to connect
My spirit
My soul
My inner wise
Spirit
That of knowing,
Hey there,
What's up

Chapter Ten
Happiness

Dear Lamplighter, let us now talk about happiness. To practice mimicking God's action is to practice offering compassion to self and others. True compassion is love. Just as God is love.

I truly understand when one is in the midst of life's challenges, it is difficult to think happiness can still be had. Compassion or no compassion. Or when one is saddened by continuous bad news.

This is what I have to offer.

We are here. We can't be denied. We can't be insignificant.

If we want a harmonious world we need to want to be a *lamplighter*. One who contributes to happiness.

A *lamplighter* knows God exists.
A *lamplighter* holds the flame lit to faith in God's plan.
A *lamplighter* therefore, does not question why, but focuses on how.

When my children were diagnosed with life-threatening conditions, some people tried to ask me about possible bad karma. I answered that I don't go there. That would be monkey mind work. I simply acknowledged that God had given me information in the past which I was able to now put into effect. Plus, He had been training me to be a *lamplighter*. So I was, in fact, able to deal with the situation; no questions, no looking back, no anger with God.

*Acceptance, Acceptance, Acceptance
with Passion*

Yes, sometimes it was very scary, frustration with medical care, great sympathy, screaming sympathy for my children. These were moments of needing some fuel for my lamp. God was the only one who could fill it at that point. That is when I could be rid of fear and reach back to focus on what is needed now.

The number one need was my need to hold the flame to happiness.

Pearls of Wisdom

The power of happiness is life fulfilling.

Fear and evil cannot live in happiness.

Love is happiness.
It is a preferred consciousness.

Hate cannot live in happiness.
Judgment cannot live in happiness.
Nor can blame, never name calling / labels.
Comparisons and criticism cannot live in happiness.

Happiness is Gratitude in Action.
How about that?

Happiness is Gratitude in Action.

When in Gratitude, there is Happiness.

Gratitude takes us to co-create with God!
How about that?
This is truth.

Fear cannot live in gratitude and happiness.

I needed to focus on my children's feelings.
By holding the flame of happiness within myself,
my hope was that they would never feel alone or alienated from me.

If I allowed even the thought of fear to enter me, then fear would begin to win.

If I say I believe in happiness, then I live it.

I dedicate my life towards a happy life,

towards having all the beings in all the world be happy.

Happiness is a beautiful thing.
A beautiful flower does not think, *"Oh, today I'll be less beautiful."*

A simple question for yourself or you may present to another:

"How may life be enriched now?"

By focusing on this question,
and not on the possibility of scariness, blame, anger, tough challenge, etc.,
happiness becomes the focus. Therefore it has the chance to win.

May We Be

May we be in all of our beings ... a lamplighter too,

Dear Lord,
we have sincere intention to work with
Light,
Your positive influence of love,
so graciously given, endlessly,

we contribute to world peace,
by reaching to:
light the flame of happiness,

as much as possible,
for each person we connect with…

I know this true
You pave the way, I live Your guarantee.

Dear Lamplighter

We feel more…
The light of love
Filling up our soul,

We then pass it on

*Always
Daily*

*Minute by minute,
Then there we are*

*Living in gratitude
and happiness…..*

How about that?

Chapter Eleven
Connecting the Dots

Okay here's the scoop. Have you ever seen those movies where someone is writing a fictional movie script which begins to become the writer's reality?

Now, have you ever had it happen to you where you're reading a book when some scenes begin to manifest in your life? And you ask, *"Now what's really going on?"*

Well, it happened to me. The first time is another layer in my becoming a God devotee after 27 years of atheism.

And…... after writing the intro to this book, I began to wonder what was going to happen to my life -- if anything -- as I figured out how to write this book. Hehe. Then I actually did begin to have experiences and interactions to help with the exact chapter I was working on.

One Day

*O*ne day I received a most wonderful connection, a powerful heavenly gift! It happened after I had written two chapters, about midway through this book. First, I wrote the chapter on connecting. Then, within a couple of weeks, I wrote the chapter on respect, honor and reverence. That evening I was quiet, feeling in awe.

The next morning was the birthday of my son who had passed several years before. I began to think of what I wanted to do, since my day was free of any schedules. I decided I didn't want to be alone, but everyone was working. I then felt a little sad and so I wondered even more. Then I wished I could get some kind of little miracle from my son. I missed him so.

Suddenly the phone rang. It was my friend Marilyn Kapp asking if I had plans and could she take me out to breakfast? She didn't have to work. Quickly my spirits lifted. What a gift! I just knew it was magical.

She even gave me a gift, a darling little package with pink and lime green wrapping with a lime green bow. It is one of my favorite color combos. She said my son directed the entire packaging and gift. He told her to use the lime green ribbon in a particular drawer. To her surprise, there was a dark green ribbon. He told her to look deeper. Sure enough, the lime green ribbon popped out with just enough length for a bow! Wow!

We would usually go to a restaurant just east of us. However, she said we were directed to go to a certain restaurant that was on the west side of town. Okay, I said. During breakfast, her son sent a text with a picture he just needed to share. It was a gorgeous large tree in full bloom, covered with pink blossoms and bright lime green leaves! Stunning! How about that! The Tree of Life.

After breakfast, she said she'd freshen up then meet me out front. *"How about where the fountain is in the little outdoor plaza?"* she asked. Okay.

As soon as I got to the fountain area, I saw that a dance performance was about to begin. They had made a little wood platform to dance on. It extended out and over the steps leading toward the fountain. Little tables and chairs surrounded the stage. So I sat down.

Little by little, as I watched performers and musicians preparing to begin the show, I realized what was about to begin, for real! What was it? Flamenco!! My all-time favorite! Flamenco dancing was my obsession for many decades!

In the many many years living in my little village, well over two decades, neither of us had ever seen a dance performance in the little plaza, nor ever heard of any -- let alone flamenco!!!

And there they were! Beautiful elegant women dressed in their gorgeous colorful dresses. Polka dots and ruffles were the theme. How I still love those glamorous outfits!

They walked around preparing. Their pride and joy was contagious! To say I was overjoyed is to minimize the ecstatic flood of emotions that were going through me! My mind was wild with the acknowledgement of what was happening, right before my eyes! A dream, an incredible, unexpected yet totally acceptable event! A dream come true!

I sat down at the outdoor cafe with a full grin from ear to ear.
I just knew I was in the middle of a connecting-the-dots miracle!

Marilyn showed up and her mouth literally dropped open, her eyes huge! She said *"What? How can this be happening?"* And, granted, Marilyn is a true medium. She said, *"Me, of all people! I can't believe this is happening! What are the chances? What a gift!"*

"And how!" I replied, as we were witnessing an entire flamenco show!! For free!

I was so excited I could hardly stand it! Then I got the urge to get up and dance. Sure enough, at that exact moment, the performing dancer walked up to me alone and asked if I wanted to join her.

"Okay," I said.

Hallelujah! Do you think I was happy?

Together we danced around and about the little outdoor plaza, 'round the fountain, 'round the folks.

We were smiling and dancing and just loving it. I was having fun! I could see Marilyn too was grinning from ear to ear!

After I finished, I walked over to her and said, *"I got to dance on Diego's birthday!"*

Marilyn answered, *"As per your Facebook post yesterday, saying your boys grew up watching you practice, Diego is now saying he gets to watch his Mama dance again for his birthday!"*

Awwwww, happy tears.

We continued our visit, relishing the presence's presents. Meaning, the bestowing of gifts right now, and continuously all morning long! I knew it was happening because of what I had just written. I was in the middle of co-creating connecting the dots, believing in it wholeheartedly, without a doubt. I was also receiving respect, honor and reverence from my son and the other spirits who were helping to connect the dots.

I said *"We are obviously in the middle of miracles happening, without doubt!"*

"Absolutely!" Marilyn answered.

A while later Marilyn said, *"We must leave now. I was just told not another word, now."*

"Okay!"

We got to the car and it had a warning ticket on it. It had a time listed to tow the car which would have been 30 minutes past our allowed time. And we had 5 minutes left before being towed! We were blessed!

The Vortex

I had been feeling a vortex around and about me, growing, expanding and filtering my space. Therefore, I felt extremely blessed and happy, and not totally surprised. Grateful indeed! Marilyn seemed more surprised.

I was debating whether to include this story in this how-to book, although it is also about me sharing some of my life. I didn't think this book was going to be about magic. And now I say to myself, but my life is all about magic, so why should I deny it?

As a child, like most everyone, magic was fun and mysterious. Something mysterious arouses my curiosity, which is something I've felt all my life. I do not believe I'm alone in this, *dear lamplighter.* I realize now that God is most austere and mysterious. Then, naturally, once I threw God away any possibility of magic disappeared also.

God made himself known to me by what I call pure magic. Therefore, magic has been a part of my life since. He knew I was basically a doubting Thomas, which I've come to realize is true of any atheist. It is the consciousness of being in an argument with God, asking for proof.

3D proof would be welcomed by anyone. Why? Because it is magical.

What I propose in writing this chapter is the possibility that you, *dear lamplighter*, will create an expandable, circulating vortex of positive compassionate energy. Having an all-encompassing, true, deep belief in its existence, therefore, and then………. You will be on its magical carpet ride. For real! Should this happen, *dear lamplighter,* please write to me about it. I'd love to hear it all.

And actually, compassion is magical! There has been many a time a client in need comes to me, consumed with fear or anger, worn out, perplexed, downtrodden only to be turned around solely through compassion.

For me to see a face go
from wrinkly fear to a bright young happy face is magical! :-}
Why?
Because one can get a wrinkly fear-based face,
not by just one hour of misery but days,
maybe months or years. What happens?

The self inflicted, sabotaging consequences of actions stimulated and remembered with sad or miserable thoughts get lifted with a passion for compassion, to bring back hope and self love going forward. Creating a new direction, a new vortex with vibrancy expressed on their sweet faces, lifting the craters of wrinkly woes.

Pearls of Wisdom

Intentionally with sincerity
Connecting Dots
To Create
a vortex for our world,
Reaching,
Searching
for a truth,
accepting too
responsibility
for our own actions,
Extending, directing
ourselves

to Connect
in *God's Web*,
His time, His way,
begins to interlock
Us
into the *3D God net*.
Swirling round and round
like a tender whirlwind,
attracting that which would
enrich our life 24/7!
This is magical!

By *Dancing Through Our Light*,
we may accomplish our mission! Fueled by God's gas pump 24/7,
recognized or not! How about that?
Why? Because,
we each have an indigenous need to connect in a loving and merciful manner.
Aww.

Thank you Dear Lord
For understanding our need

Far beyond our wildest dreams
You alone know what awaits
Death lurking round every corner
we do not know
not aware
not a clue.

Then recognize a life
we cherish.

Now asking You
Assistance true,
we love
we need
kindness too.
For understanding the
Depth you seek for us.
Not to be seen easily.
Therefore never leave us,
I know this true.

But, a reason known, somewhere
I do declare, I have great Need
here on earth, to beg Thee
Never leave, Dear Lord.
I know this true,
my humanness needs connection,
Consciously,

Bring on that Magic!
I await Thee.

Part III

Chapter Twelve
The Art of Passion for Compassion

Little by little as our awareness grows, we understand even more the power of the word.

By thinking of our dialog as an art, we may use the dialog as a tool brush to paint out our life. What would you like to paint? And how does it work? Let's start with some mirror work.

Who am I anyway?
In order to paint the self portrait, I can 'see' myself by understanding what motivates me (needs) and what I am feeling. I then have tools to paint my scene with a feeling which is being expressed through my heart and soul.

To ask and answer: *"What am I feeling?"* This is the first stroke across the canvas. Hmm.
To ask and answer: *"Why did I do that or say that?"* This question is searching for the direction of the stroke across the canvas, which is the need. The answers to these two questions paints the actual canvas that others see. How about that?

How do we perceive ourself?
Who is that masked person in the mirror?

We have been painting out our entire life with:
(1) our emotions/feelings and…
(2) our motivations/actions/needs.

Now we need more details.

What did I do with that feeling? What color did I paint it?
What shape did the emotion take on?

Let's remember the hidden agendas. Ha!
We may think we know what scene is being painted but it proves to be only partial. There are a lot of scenes in the background we don't notice because they were painted a while back.

For example, I have a plan to paint a certain scene. Then suddenly there is interference. Never would I think that something in the background scene could cause the present interference. I may think it's obvious that someone else is to blame.

This is where we can then get angry or anxious. We may give in to fear and hopelessness, thinking the odds are against us.

Hidden agendas prevent us from going where we want to go and
can attract things we end up cringing over,
painting a scene unwanted.

When several hidden agendas surface or clash with another person's hidden agenda it may seem like a bomb explosion. At that point, we respond violently to our own self. Dislike and self-sabotage can happen within minutes. It may continue for a long time or kick in here and there.

What does my painting look like then? What can I do?

Go back to the beginning.
Just remember, what is God's action?
What color does He use?
Time to pull out the color of love
with endless mercy to me.

Mercy Mercy! What is it? What color is it?
Patience, sometimes tolerance, forgiveness.
Forgiveness on so many levels.
If I must forgive someone, including myself,
then I must have judged. Then I must forgive myself for judging.

Mercy Mercy!
It is also acceptance, on so many levels.
Mercy also allows for the time to get it right.

When in misery,
use it as an opportunity to realize
the *need to connect* in a loving and merciful manner to 'me'.

Who else besides 'me' is going to take me out of misery?
How do I get out of it? What can I do? Time to ask:

What's going on inside of me? For real!
1.) What am I feeling?
2.) What am I thinking?
3.) What am I really needing?

These first two points have been crucial for me in bringing in the awareness I needed to change my life! Theoretically I understood the difference between the two questions. Differentiating the definition of thinking and feeling made me search and understand the exact meaning of the words. Then I could answer the third question: what am I needing that produced this feeling?

This seemingly simple process was the beginning of unscrambling these sneaky hidden agendas within me. And most importantly, it gave me a mental path I could work with to get myself out of a deep hole. Not only emotionally, but to change my entire world physically and financially. I went from Ha! to Aha!

It may be helpful to add:
1.) What am I feeling? *What color is it?*
2.) What am I thinking? *What shape is it taking on?*

3.) What needs are playing out? *What is the framework of the painting?*
4.) What are my hidden agendas? *Let me step back so I can see the whole painting.*

I think it best to tell you the story of my first encounter with this process because it did turn on a great light bulb for me.

Turn on the Light, Please

The nonviolent counselor asked me something. I don't remember what. I made a statement: "When my husband left I felt abandoned". I had gone to see this counselor to help with my two teenage sons to get them to wash the dishes. Somehow the counselor turned the conversation to my marriage. Though we had not divorced legally, it had been almost seven years of separation and we had agreed upon a plan to make it legal.

I didn't think I had any hidden agendas on the subject. I had been on a conscious spiritual path. I had done my processing. I was into the present and had hope for the future. I was not angry. The fear of being alone was long past. I was feeling courageous and uplifted.

So, why did the counselor bring up the past? Marriage? It was over. I was satisfied in that department.

Naturally, being the sensitive that I am, opening up the topic of abandonment put me right back there and this guy was trying to convince me that my husband did not abandon me/us.

Yeah right! Did I feel the surge within my solar plexus begin to raise its dragon fire? Yes! Of course he abandoned me. What do you mean he didn't?!! I tell you he did!

Little by little the counselor showed me my hidden agenda and the self inflicted sabotaging consequences thereof. I'll spell out what led to the basic insight.

For years I told myself the 'fact' of being abandoned. This made me feel lousy, sometimes angry, but always lousy. Since it was put on me, I could never erase it. One heavy layer about it was the 'fact' that he chose to abandon me and our children. This fact made me feel weak for years. I had no power over it but to accept it and move on. I felt a wedge of weakness had been hammered into me if I thought about it. So I moved on. I had to function. I had to get a new life. I had to compromise with myself. I had to accept it if I wanted a happy life and to move on.

The counselor eventually explained to me that the 'fact' of abandonment is not a feeling. It is an interpretation of an action. To abandon is not a feeling. I can't *feel* abandoned. I *can feel* scared, lonely, disheartened, hopeless. I can feel fragile and mortified and lonely…. **These are emotions. I can deal with emotions. I can work with emotions.**

Feeling abandoned? I can't work with that.
Scared or fragile- I can work on this and become brave.
Lonely- I can work on this and make friends, and I can even get married again.
Mortified- I can work on this and become happy.

Disheartened- kind of like losing courage. Through this I can become brave, even about bringing in love once more. This is a good word for describing our feelings that come from any thoughts of betrayal. This is what we feel. It infers that somehow my heart feels less full of love, as if some love were sucked out of me, and yet I **can** figure out how to fill it up, again.

To recognize the **real** feelings going through me is very good work,
and may even be enjoyable work!

Yes, an enjoyable work really worth doing!
This really is **soul time work!**

Abandonment is something done to me, therefore to focus on my 'feelings' of abandonment, does not help me to get out of the discomfort. It's more of a label, not a feeling. When I told myself I felt abandoned, I told myself without saying the actual words: "Woe is me, it can't be erased. It can't be healed. I can only accept it and move on." There was a constant sense of shame that could not be worked with, that I could not get rid of.

We <u>can</u> work with our emotions.
Why?
They are something inside of us.
We are born with feelings.
We react to every feeling whether we acknowledge it or not.
It is basic.
It is indigenous.
It is real.
How about that?

****

Dear Lamplighter, I have found that abandonment issues seem to be strong in our society. How about you? Do you agree? This is why I thought it a good topic to show us the power of words.

Abandonment has become a label that has shame as a consequence.
It may indicate someone was not loved, is not loved, and therefore cannot be loved.
Abandonment issues are examples of a story getting scrambled with a feeling.

We have a lot of words in our English language. What I have learned by practicing nonviolence is to, **please, *I beg myself,*** pay attention to the words I use to describe anything. They are powerful!

Words trigger emotions which may push unwanted action.

In other words, what have I *really* been painting?

Finally I came to the conclusion that not only must I pay attention to the words I use, but also drop some words from my vocabulary. I ask, "*Why were words invented? To communicate?*" Yet some words are meant to be mean. Or are they? Is the definition meant to hurt or is it our interpretation? Oh my!

Can we take a nice, joyful word and trigger ill feelings? What tone of voice am I using? What's my body language? Eye expression? Hate or love in my face? Tolerance or joy?

For real, am I being honest? What am I really talking about? Am I telling myself a lie, thinking it is true? Oh dear, oh my, what real 'fact' did I do unto me?

"I feel abandoned" or "I was abandoned" is a lie, an untruth. Living with it as if it were a 'fact', was making me feel bad, vulnerable, depleted, ashamed, guilty.

****

Let's talk about this.
There are three points to my story as to how I hurt myself with the word 'abandon'.

To summarize, **the first point** is: <u>I told a lie to myself</u>, while thinking it was a fact: that I *felt* abandoned. Therefore I told myself to 'own' the word 'abandon' as a *feeling*, as if it were a part of my being. I was not aware.

And yet, the truth was that I was owning a label. What I felt was scared. You, me, all of us cannot *feel* abandoned. It was a thought form in my brain, not in my heart, which triggered ill feelings in my heart. This, then, made my whole being feel ill.

We <u>can</u> change our thoughts; opinions, judgments, criticism, labels, etc.

The second point is about <u>interpretations</u>: I told myself another lie by thinking it was a fact that he abandoned me. I cannot speak for him. It was not a fact. I interpreted his action. Speaking up for someone else is always going to be an interpretation, one way or the other. This is truth.

Remember I said a huge, bad, horrifying layer to my abandonment issue was that my husband had chosen to abandon us? It was like a brick on my head and chest.

Special Note Dear Lamplighter.
When we are repeating someone's story, let's clarify it. *"This is the way I heard it." "This is the way I see it".* In some way, making sure it is understood that it may not be a fact or the whole story. I need to clarify it to myself and others. **This truly helps to be aware.** Aware of how our words may affect us. All of us.

An interpretation of an action generally takes us to live in the untruth. Which can then create more hidden agendas. Ha! Oh dear! He did choose to leave. It was my choice to use the word abandon and own all of its interpretations. Holy Moly! What was I doing to my own self?

As the counselor explained the interpretation theory to me,
I then began to remove the brick.
How about that?

As I began to agree with the counselor,
I began to own the real truth and then I could actually feel the weight being lifted.
Actually, I had been owning me abandoning my own self. Oh dear! Oh my!

Until we check it out, we live under interpretations!

*****

The Real Truth is,
We are always a person.
Who is experiencing life on earth
through
feelings, actions, words and thoughts.
That's it!

*****

It still amazes me some 15 years later that a bunch of words could change my world…. in…… one….. hour.

Now to continue the story...
The counselor said, *"Generally people don't leave something or someone."*

"Really?"

"No, they focus on going somewhere".

Really? Well, that makes sense as to how someone can justify a hurtful decision and action. Aha! I thought he had given me a strong clue.

He continued, *"If you ask him if he abandoned you, I bet he'd say, no he didn't."*

Well, yes, he had already done that because I had already accused him of abandonment. He answered, *"No way!"* Can we agree he left? Yes!

As long as I accused, he defended himself. We'd get nowhere. I was trying to get him to see the enormous pain we were in, which I said he caused by leaving.

I was interpreting and labeling his action. Why did I not understand my interpretation of his action would come across as an accusation? Because I was focused on my agenda of truth and responsibility. Therefore my anger drowned out any agenda of needing to connect.

I was telling him what he was doing and I was saying he was wrong. I labeled his action. I was trying to paint his painting. I said that I knew he had planned to abandon us. So, who would say yes? He said no!

"It's human nature!" my dad would say, when finding no rhyme or reason as to why or what motivates a person to take an action unwanted by others, and maybe even himself. As if there was no control!

******

Pearl of Wisdom

To recognize this, is a big deal!
If I say I cannot control myself; someone or something made me do it,
time to ask, what do I need?
What need is not being met?

Sita Paloma

If someone tells me that another made 'em do it,
time to ask, what is their need? What are they really feeling?

But in a way, I agree with my dad, because these uncontrolled actions have been common throughout history, one may say it's natural. We were trained without realizing it. We have developed the opinion and thoughts that we all do uncontrollable actions; that they just happen. This somehow justifies our actions or claims it as "common sense".

This then leads us to the next point.

The third point. <u>Hidden Agendas</u>. <u>Ha!</u> Hidden agendas that just hang out and sit in the background scenes.

We can have a conscious desire
to figure out what our unmet need is,
that triggered the opinion,
judgment, criticism, labeling, motivation, justification,
and make a decision to change.

We then stop allowing some unconscious part of us to take action,
we stop the hidden agendas - stop the uncontrollable me. Ha!

We can take over that paint brush and paint our canvas!
This is the Big Wow!! Aha!

An interpretation that I made a while back, can become a hidden agenda popping out in the present, right now. Example: like an old rationalized story getting scrambled with the present story creating a justification or a blame.

In my case, the Ha! was to keep my focus on a type of blame for my discomfort. It was too scary to own the feeling of being scared. It was normal to say something in my life made me feel inferior or sad. It fueled a little anger always, subtly, opening a path to guilt, shame and blame.

This hidden agenda, that of keeping my focus on a type of blame for my discomfort, was safer and normal. Feelings can be scary and we don't understand why. It may be safer to feel anger. Scrambled stories, rationalizations and feelings are what we live by. Oh dear, oh my!

Another hidden agenda was *my* interpretation of a baby being abandoned. It meant the baby was thrown aside, without a care. This interpretation led me to feel, to paint myself as an 'abandonment', something thrown to the side without a care.

To label myself was more normal, also. Although if asked back then, I'd say I was free of self labeling.

The label of abandonment also kept me thinking, in a most subtle manner, that I needed to be dependent, like an infant. And that my children needed to be dependent on their father also. Therefore, owning the label kept me from seeing myself as capable, and kept me weak for my children. It was far from the truth!

Actually, abandonment is the summary of the action verb, to abandon or release. As in, "as a result of the abandonment the baby was adopted." Something positive. How about that?

And maybe the baby was stolen, not abandoned. Even if the baby was abandoned, we tend to assume that the baby was tossed away without a care. There have been numerous paintings showing a different scene. Great agony comes with the need to give up a baby. This is always true. No matter the circumstance, there is always agony. Let us reach out with the intention of healing and good will.

A baby is a human being, forever a beautiful gift. A baby can never be a thing, like an abandonment. A heavenly human baby was left on the doorstep. Awww.

If we lived in a world with a limited vocabulary, abandonment would never even be conceived. People would automatically become enthralled, excited with a found baby, wanting desperately to care for the baby with gratitude. There could never be a thought that the baby was lost or thrown away by someone! The focus would stay on the infant in the present. Not in the past, and with no thoughts or judgments of who did what to the baby. This is a Big Deal! Vibrations go out.

A human is a human, forever a heavenly gift!

Pearl of Wisdom
Once we reach maturity,
there cannot be an abandonment by someone else to us.
We are no longer a dependent. We become in charge of our own destiny.
Thank you.
Therefore we must become aware.

If we want a different future, or more love in our life, let's check out our own paintings. *Dear Lamplighter,* by processing what colors and brush strokes are needed for the canvas, we can paint a different background, one that is more supporting of who we may want to be. Really be! Really!

May I?

Really be! Really be!
may I really be
that one,
that soul,
who's always nagging me
      to,
really be! really be!
really be me?

Chapter Thirteen
What ambiance do I want?

What ambiance do I want for my painting, right now? What feelings do I want to feel? What colors do I want to offer the world? What colors am I using now?

If I am using a strong bold color like red, can I express it safely, so the paint on the brush and canvas does not drip where I don't want it to or override and unbalance the picture? Heaven knows I do not want to paint and manifest the same unwanted scene again in my life.

Let us understand that a person's reaction,
the direction of the paintbrush stroke,
is always
a response to a need pushed by feelings
going on inside.
Whether the response is to someone else or to my own thinking.

May I repeat this, please:

May we understand that any person's reaction,
the direction of the paintbrush stroke,
is always
a response to a need within,
pushed by feelings going on inside.

The need yields the motivation- the paint brush stroke,
to take action- the direction of the stroke,
triggered by emotional feelings.

So then, what am I actually feeling and thinking? What do I need to give myself to be able to connect and respond compassionately? Even to myself, especially to myself.

**Time to pick up a new toolbox,
stock it full of different colors/feelings and store it in the mind.**

I may then identify what I am feeling.
And with practice,

upon receiving an accusation or hearing something unjust or uncomfortable,
I may then identify a feeling
without
my former scrambled hidden agendas and without going into rationalizations,
without interpretations and stories.
Yahoo!

**Distinguishing my feelings from all other thoughts
gives me the proper tools to begin to unscramble hidden agendas
which keeps me from responding with compassion to all parties.**

I need to hear what I am feeling in order to know what I can do to enrich my life!

The mind goes around and around, searching for something to hold on to which ends up being a whole story/rationalization rather than an emotion. This, then, becomes a hidden agenda popping out from the background.

Our mind travels so very fast that we do not realize what is really being expressed. We think we are in the present moment understanding what's going on. But our reaction includes a piece of our history.

Therefore, at times of great challenge, I allow my soul to take a hold and
ask,
What am I feeling and what do I need to do to change?

This is the first step to self empathy.

Self Empathy is the shift of consciousness to hear our own soul.
by asking, what am I thinking and feeling?

I give myself empathy by:
* hooking up my God connection (tuning-in to my higher consciousness)
* acknowledging my feelings
* identifying my needs
*giving myself some mercy time
* and choosing an emotion that I prefer to surface

**Taking the steps, the action to change
my emotion,
a feeling unwanted
changes my whole story, my entire life. Guaranteed!**

A Little Addition.

Dear Lamplighter, when my manuscript was complete, I gave a copy to my brother, Victor Villaseñor, who's a professional writer. Hehe! He was able to offer me the further editing I needed. He's become my writing teacher. One of his suggestions was to save a portion of the Buddha story for later. Because the story had information about Buddha's emotions, I knew the deleted portion would be appropriate later on.

"As he (Buddha) had been mumbling, he finally spoke clearly, telling me to take the briefcase and of his woes...

His brow of anger dropped as it shifted to being perplexed.

His anger had only surfaced for a few seconds as we argued. When we met, though he was feeling overwhelmed, upset, fed up, exhausted, disgusted, he did not have a drip of anger. He was also delighted with life, extremely optimistic, determined, feeling 100% self worth and worthy, creating solid confidence in his will, certain of his knowing there is an answer.

These were his woes. All of these emotions, with the exception of anger, were within him constantly. He finally made the decision to leave the castle because of his feelings.

He did not have anger like we experience. We hold on to anger because we think we have no control over the situation. He definitely was a prince of some sort. He had never experienced ordinary life. He never had a situation he had no control over while growing up. He only knew freedom and delight.

Therefore it was impossible to retain a feeling of anger for more than a few seconds. And even then, his anger held a desire to be expressed quickly, vocally. It did not have the capacity to sit in his body. He was blessed that way."

The Buddha left his life in the castle because of how he felt.
The searching on how to change what we feel,
changes our life.
Guaranteed!

Dear Lamplighter, sometimes we do need to change our surroundings, or actually move. Sometimes we need to change our attitude and our mental dialogue. Bottom line, our thoughts need to change, in order for our feelings to change.

To be real, to know what is really going on inside of us.
We've got to drop the blame, shame, guilt and control, interpretations, labels, expectations, sarcasm and judgments; what am I forgetting? We then can get to our own bottom line, our truth, what is real inside: personal feelings and personal needs. Note: a personal need is, "I need…" or "I need to do…". It cannot be, "I need him or her to do…". We drop the illusions.

Then make a request.
What would enrich my life?

Make a request to myself.
Make a request to another.

The Buddha requested to remove himself from his protected surroundings
in order to find truth,
to enrich his life.

Once he was there,
knowing his truth and owning his preferred emotions,
his connection to God, he was then able to go anywhere.

So with us,
finding the truth about our emotions
is key
to know our path and our needs.
This is truth.
Guaranteed!

How about that!

A Prayer

Dear Lord,
May we surface
that which we know is true,
the color of love with all its mercy?
I know it's true
deep within
those walls of loneliness,
at times making me
the color of sadness.
Only to realize then there I may
use my mind with its discernment.
What is real?
What is true?
Me, dear Lord.
I know deep within,
I am but a
reflection of You!

In all Your Glory!
May I witness too
The longing I have,
That urgency
To
Reach out and
be touched?
I am but a creature
here on Earth.
What do I hear?
That Love, Your Love
Encircling me with its
Radiant Golden Bubbles of Love,
once more I feel
the effervescence with the color of love.
Mercy has it once more.
May I love me now, completely.

Chapter Fourteen
Capture the Ability to Feel What I Wanna Feel

To practice the Art of Bringing Emotions to the Surface, that is feelings that are within me, continues to teach my mind and heart how to work together to express what I need in a more compassionate and *complete* manner. The colors I choose have more purpose and vibrancy.

Sweet self empathy is the process I need to hear what I am feeling in order to know what I can do to change the feeling and bring a preferred emotion to the surface.

Then when responding, I have a better chance to do so with compassion. This practice stops the monkey mind and the destructive chaos. It may then keep me free of despair, chaos and destruction on a regular basis.

Why? What actually happens when confronted with an uncomfortable situation is that my body reacts with a feeling, fueling an emotion. My brain receives information about some hidden agendas but my mind doesn't have a file on how or what to do compassionately. My mind will quickly mix up, scramble up an emotion with a rationalization and its story.

The response I give and then receive only fuels the storm or misunderstandings. Frustration comes in, which may continue to mix up even more emotions and rationalizations, plus the present information. Thus the scramble continues and I don't even realize it.

Best to be able to bring a desired feeling to the surface rather than be stuck in overwhelming emotions then reacting to the same or similar scenes. What is being painted now?

La Novela

Please allow me to compare this with flamenco dancing. Hehe.
In order for the foot tapping to sound like music, I would need to practice a sequence of foot taps made by my toe, heel and flat foot. Then I'd shift my body weight to include taps on the other foot. If each tap did not have a distinct sound, I would not produce the music desired, it would be muffled. The timing is also crucial to producing the tune.

This is a big deal! A Grande Big Deal!
By allowing my body to feel the different emotions, with empathy,
it can then distinguish what is really going on! Finally!

Differentiating clearly,
my rational mind with all its stories and hidden agendas
from my actual physical feelings.

Ha! Each hidden agenda stimulates an emotion. Therefore, when confronted, I could immediately have a basket full of emotions, which are being stimulated and fueled by numerous feelings, triggered by thoughts going on in my mind.

By recognizing and distinguishing each feeling, my mind has the freedom to then truly do its proper dance. It separates us from our attachment to an emotion that may be stimulated by an unwanted feeling. It allows us to be a witness to our own dance. Yahoo! And… this is especially true with myself when alone with my monkey mind.

To distinguish and hear each foot tap, each feeling, I can then stop the muffled sound, stop the hidden agenda which might create a new, undesired, out of tune, conversation.

Best to deal with one feeling at a time, one tap at a time, rather than creating a whole telenovela! A Mexican soap opera! Have you ever watched a *telenovela*?

When my dear sister-in-love joined our family, she remarked one day in laughter the humor she found in the similarity in the English soap operas and the Mexican *telenovelas*, which are about the drama queens and kings within us, popping out from the background scenes with their hidden agendas and secrets, wreaking havoc.

The *telenovelas* express more exasperation, more drama, louder music, all expressing their woes in great fuss n' muss and can be great entertainment!

We go wild within, being all stimulated by our emotions. Just like in a dance performance practiced true, the expression can be powerful, stimulating to the point of tears. By raising an arm in strong gesture with a foot tap and stomp, along with a snap of the fingers and eyes glaring, the flamenco dance performer can express an entire *novela* and story with its drama and expression. Then she can turn quickly, flaring up the long dragging tail of the flamenco dress, exposing a bit of its under ruffles and colors.

The *novela* continues, then, as the dancer pulls out a hidden colorful fan to wave through the air in fluid harmony, along with song and foot tapping. With desire to change the tune, she then sways her fan to cover her smile, highlighting her eyes, switching the glaring expression to the brightness of sweet love and acceptance. A full story then told true. This is life!

So too, with our verbal expression.
We can offer what is really going on inside, our feelings, needs, and requests
to share our real life, what really matters.

Share it with ourselves, owning our truth. Share what we need with others in a clear manner, distinguishing each movement, each thought from feelings, offering safety to watch and hear the dance/conversation no matter how strong the *novela* is.

The conversation may be the stormy type, it might even get a little heated up or spill great amounts of fear, and still have compassion. Compassion expresses a meaningful, thoughtful and uplifting conversation, connecting and hearing what is going on now, in this life, soul to soul.

What's Up

May I express,
 what I really feel?
And what I may need
 as a result?
It has nothing
 to do with you.

No no
 This is my feeling.
 This is my dance.
 Your words or actions
 may have triggered,
 this emotion inside,

but there's something,
something inside of me
that feels now
vulnerable and maybe angry.

But wait!
Was it not
just minutes

past when
my emotions
were just fine?

My ego draws
near, questioning
once more,
What's up?

May I offer
mercy
and make a
request?

Soul to Soul

How do we
enhance our
lives?
What's really important
right now?

Chapter Fifteen
Fourth Point, Labels

Becoming aware **of self-labeling is also needed to choreograph the dance.**
When we truly dance, we just dance. There's no thought of who we may be.

There is actually a fourth point to my self-inflicting, self-sabotaging, by simply using the word abandon and that is: self-labeling. This diminishes our self-worth or keeps us in a box. Labeling others increases alienation. When we prefer to connect, all alienation has got to go away. Any type of labeling is like kicking up the spurs in the tango dance.

Because I had anger, fear and ignorance at the time of my separation from my first husband, accepting the feeling of abandonment as a truth led me to develop it as a label over time, even though I no longer had anger towards the ex hubby or fear of living. Yet, I lived with the label, and the feelings of guilt and shame, constantly minimizing myself.

Did I even recognize that I had labeled myself, and that I was making myself feel bad? No.

I was living with the "truth" that I was shamed for being abandoned. Without awareness, this thought could not be erased.

But in fact I was giving myself a rationalization, a conclusion that I was an abandonment without saying it out loud! Again, I truly thought this was something that I could not change.

The truth of my self-labeling was shocking because there was no more anger for my ex hubby. We could sit for hours in comfortable conversation, (still can) yet I was living with emotions of guilt and shame, trying to deny it! How about that?!

This self-labeling also, somehow, gave into a labeling that I was a shamed woman, like an ashamement to society. Again like a thing, a thing to be tossed around without a care. A disgrace that has permanency because marriage is supposed to be permanent. Oooh nooo! Holy Moly! How we can maim ourselves without awareness! How about that?

How did I figure out I had an issue with abandonment? Whenever I heard talk of abandonment I'd have a quick memory of my own experience and feel a something in my gut. This no longer exists.

As I reached for a new truth with the counselor, the dark shadow, the brick, the shame, the guilt, the deep sadness began to float away. I began to paint a new, healthier scene, and ... slowly came to do the happy dance.

After the session with the counselor, I sat back in my car paralyzed with amazement. I could only release it with some tears. Then I said to myself, *"By learning how to have a conversation like that, I could love again. I would feel safe. Safe within the relationship and safe in keeping me, me."*

In conclusion, with hubby number one, we did make a settlement two years after I met the compassionate counselor. Using the compassionate tools I learned, we were able to stay in compassion. Even though he hired a lawyer, each of us was able to come out winning! Yay!

Because I felt safe with using the compassionate communication tools I learned, there was no need to hire a lawyer.

By becoming conscious of the *art of passion for compassion,* and unlocking hidden agendas, today I would've said,

"I really regret you have a need to leave me and your family. I want to accept it but I'm having a hard time. I'm scared and I have needs too. I see fear and sadness in our kids and don't know how to fix it and wish I could. What do you suggest?"

With this opening statement I am talking about my needs and feelings without accusations yet speaking my real truth.

I had a great need back then to express my discomfort. Plus, I had a need to see if there was a chance for my husband and children's dad, to own up to some responsibilities toward us. I did not want to accept his truth about needing to leave, especially with regard to dropping our financial needs. I had a lot of anger besides fear. Therefore, if I wanted a compassionate conversation, I would know not to express my anger which may fuel the dragon's fire within, rather to focus on the possibility of finding a resolution to ease my children's pain and mine, too.

Although my request would have been a bit bold, to stay in empathy to myself, I would and could not hold him responsible going forward to do anything. He had already left his full responsibility behind. He painted a new scene. Therefore I could only suggest he do something.

**Without accusations or expectations
I could then empower myself by staying
focused
on my own personal needs and feelings.**
Rather than focusing on accountability and all its shame.
Which would leave focus on something I truly have no control over.

This is a Big Wow!
I stay empowered by my positive focus!

****

Because we had so much at stake and our children were young, I did refuse to get an immediate divorce, which he honored. I believed he would help me after he had his new career.

Accepting the belief that he would help later on stopped the stress I had regarding accountability.

Then I was able to put my attention on holding on to our assets, getting a new life and stopping that particular stress. But because I had no real compassionate speaking tools for myself, my monkey mind was too wild, constantly depleting my self-worth even though I had plenty of energy to change my life.

In time I came to know it was our destiny to separate. When we made the settlement, I had come to many resolutions and was developing a new career. I had no idea that I had such abilities in myself until I began to search for a different life. And.... little by little, I actually began to have compassion for my first husband and empathy for his pain, as I reached in to hear his deeper story.

Today, if we need to be in touch, there is love, harmony and peace, knowing we are there for each other in great times of need. This has been tried and proven!

Chapter Sixteen
Searching for Truth

It is easy to stay ignorant of truth when we are clueless as to our hidden agendas. Forever I am searching and learning, unlocking these truths behind my secret doors. Doors I don't even know exist.

Dear Lamplighter, has anyone not developed a strong self critique and labels?

Actually, critiques and labels are untruths. We are not meant to be something to critique. How about that? We are someone. We are not labels. Which 'untruths' are simply hanging out in the background scenes, wreaking havoc? Maybe even a little havoc? Unnoticed, yet to be noted?

This is the big question we ponder. As a human, this is a continuous underlying search. *Who am I?*

> Remember: we are human,
> a being on a journey,
> experiencing
> feelings, actions, words and thoughts.

Someone who may think of themselves as a *something* is living an untruth.
I am not dumb, I am not smart.
I am not a stupid thing, I am not a straight A student.
I am not a victim, I am not a thug.
"I am what I am and all that I am." Popeye.

A bit more about interpretations, labels and hidden agendas.

By learning to distinguish feelings from all other thoughts, little by little we hear a deeper self, a deeper truth. How's this for an example? Because of our language, we get trained to think of ourselves as the subject in a sentence. How about that? Once we begin to listen, we discover.

Here's a good example of our languaging. *The girl is sad.* We say this as a truth. We were trained to interpret the sentence as: the sad girl. We then end up living under an interpretation! It is not a reality, nor is it a truth.

To make the girl sad is a lie, an untruth! She is a person feeling sad. How about that? Feelings change and evolve.

Why is this a big deal? Let us check out the sentence: the girl was victimized. Eventually it is interpreted as: the girl is a victim. Eventually the girl, a real person, is subtly taught to own the word 'victim' as her label, as who she is, her identity, unable to think otherwise.

We are not a subject. We are human. Yess!

There is a huge difference between the victim - and - the person was victimized. How about that?!

This is also a good example of how our everyday language scrambles a story with feelings and creates an interpretation. Oh dear! Oh my! Does this make sense?

**Interpretations and labels
can sneak into our mind on a regular basis without even realizing it.**

We know this is true. Labels are used as some of the most destructive weapons. Why? They trigger insult and injury. They are a judgment and keep us bound to the past and a slave to the future! Holy Moly!

This is one reason Dr. Marshall Rosenberg named his first book <u>Non-violence</u>. Everyday words that seem normal may take us to the point of inflicting pain. Oh dear. How about that?

By becoming aware of our thoughts, we can stop destructive consequences.

****

Let us remember this sweet mantra.
Love Always, hurt never!
Practice words without spurs
then dance.

By practicing: *What am I feeling?* labels and interpretations begin to diminish naturally. And naturally we are then connecting and communicating with our soul. Which becomes our norm.

Help Us

Help us to educate ourselves,
Dear Lord
To understand the power of words.
Combined with intention,
body language and the
potential dragon within,

I know and understand
the volatile potential of their vibration.

With Your continuous help
I know I can
tune into a vibration
whose state is that of compassion.
Ready to love all serve all.
Thank you

Chapter Seventeen
Practicing the Dance

Ask yourself: "What am I feeling and what is the need behind my feeling?" I feel…I need….
Examples:
I feel hungry. I need to eat.
It is normal for us to say, "I am hungry." To <u>become aware of physical feelings</u>, for a while say to yourself, "*I feel … "*.

Because we have so many details in our lives, we tend to think about a 'something' first, rather than being aware of what we are feeling/being.

This practice is to acknowledge a physical something going on inside of me. Like what feeling is alive in me right now? Allow yourself to feel it. In this case, feeling hunger is also a way to acknowledge that an appetite is developing.

The Appetite

My papa was an admirable man. That is many folks admired him, his personality and his accomplishments.

What I can say is that he presented clearly, a persona of great confidence and expressed his love of life through his wonderful admiration of people.

How he'd take the time to discern and discuss admirable traits, characteristics in a person.

Remembering a time as a child, one day when we were out and about he said to me,

"See that fellow over there? See the pride he has in the way he walks? Even though he's only pumping gas, you know he's a man of top-quality! Someone you may trust to get the job done in a dignified manner. He's good to his children, he puts them first and he's loyal to his wife."

And how he loved and admired his horses! Papa was a horseman. He loved to watch them eat. He loved that they showed great appetite and when they'd chew, it sounded so *sabroso* (extra tasty).

My papa enjoyed sharing his thoughts and feelings at dinner time. Papa was a storyteller.

He expressed great admiration for anyone who came to visit by having sincere interest in who they were!

Then he'd share his bounty by feeding them. First by expressing the love and admiration he had for his wife, our mama. He talked about the great feast that was soon to be, and her savory cooking talents, building up their appetite.

For he said having a good appetite is everything! Meaning everything in life.

Papa loved to feel hunger. He would find delight in acknowledging the hunger pains with knowing the food is coming. It welcomed the appetite, he'd say.

After dinner, while waiting for dessert, he'd shower his guests with fun storytelling using humor and animation. Through his admiration of life, he'd fill his guests with an abundance of love.

Papa was a *lamplighter*. He reached for uplifting conversation with great interest in the meaning of life. He had a passion for compassion, and a good appetite!

How To Practice This New Dance

Developing Two Important Steps Is the Key We Need for Expansion

First Step.
By practicing this simple everyday menu, that of acknowledging needs and feelings, the mind will begin to naturally and easily expand to acknowledge how different hidden agendas were developed, without any fear. Why? The mind, in its natural state, that of freedom and expansion, will only bring out information that can be handled, right now! Truly, truly.

Second Step.
As I allow myself to actually have more awareness of the different emotions/feelings that I am experiencing throughout the day, I receive more heart expansion. Truly, truly.

Examples:
I feel hungry. I need to eat.
I feel happy and need to celebrate.

I feel ambitious and need schooling.
I feel inspired and need to write.

A Passion for Compassion

I feel angry. I need to deal with this, or
I need to talk.

I feel angry. What do I need?
Right now I need to release some tension, I'll go scrub some pots and pans.

I feel annoyed, I need some uplifting.
I feel restricted and agitated. I need expansion.

I feel discouraged. I need encouragement.
I feel vulnerable, I need to think about how to deal with the request.

I feel tired and lazy. I need to rest.
I feel moved (emotionally). I need to give gratitude.

**We can work with feelings at any time, any place, anywhere.
We can change how we feel. Yes!!!**

**It is within our capacity as humans to change our thoughts and feelings by choosing to do so.
The key we need is to ask ourselves for compassion, with sincerity in our heart.**

Another big deal! We know this deep inside! We cannot change how someone else feels! Sometimes this is A Big Sigh! And so true. We cannot paint their canvas! We may send blessings. One may react to us with a certain color, but the one is still holding their own paintbrush.

*As *lamplighters* we know this.
*As *lamplighters* we want to exemplify
surfacing the feeling needed for a compassionate conversation.

With the Love of God and Our Higher Self, we can do this. This is doable, and adore-able.

Practicing this dance performance with ourselves, regularly, rewards us with the ability to go there, in empathy, when needed. Such as with accusations or complex conversations requiring response.

****

The reverse may be practiced also; I need……..and feel……..about it.

Examples:

I need to go to work and I feel excited.
I need to make a good impression and feel anxious.

I want to hear you and I need to stay on schedule and feel scared to miss my appointment.
I need to pay attention. I missed out and feel furious!

I need to wash the dishes and I feel lazy and tired.
I need my lunch hour to run an errand. This thought now makes me feel encouraged to finish my work promptly.

I need to get up and stretch. I feel lethargic.
I need to go get groceries. I feel happy.

I need to walk the dog. I feel grateful to have him/her in my life.
I need support right now, I am feeling a lack of confidence.

I need to shout with joy because I feel so amazed!
I need to get there on time and feel nervous.

I need to give thanks. I feel so grateful.
I need to prepare because I feel hopeful.

I need to release some tension because I feel too much anger.

There is need *to* note that sometimes, we need to recognize, that the real me needs to forget about it all and just sit with uncomfortable feelings for a while to get through it, all of it, gut wrenched, monkey mind stimulus, drama and strong overwhelming emotions.

This is also true with too much bliss! Haha! But so true! We need to get through it, overwhelming emotions, to get on with the day.

You may be saying, "*What?!*" right now, thinking, "*Yeah, right, I'm gonna feel bliss? Just demand it of myself? Don't think so…*"

Pearls of Wisdom

Please remember:
happiness is a state of consciousness
besides making the decision to want to be happy right now.

We deal with our emotions/feelings 24/7. Continuous happiness is foreign to us.
Therefore,

I need to be aware of what I am feeling right now,
acknowledge it fully, and sit with that feeling for a while.
I need to own it, in order to experience it, to get through it.

Then I can get onto the next emotion, feel it, get through it.

Eventually the I AM,
the human I am, will want to bring on happiness and even bliss if allowed!
This is truth! Each of us was born with this ability!
How about that?

This is the journey our soul is wanting to talk about.
Sometimes it is like a conspiracy by our soul and ego, to get us to that bliss,
that is, to be in tune!

Yes, at times we are dealing with something which is disturbing. And it is what we are really wanting and possibly needing. Why? Because not dealing with it would be even greater misery! Therefore, we can still be conscious of being happy, even grateful to have the chance to deal with the situation. It is good when we can help. Help someone, help ourselves. We stay focused on being in tune! Therefore it can feel good by acknowledging our worth and abilities. Giving continuous gratitude! Yes!!!

If we truly want a humanitarian world, we truly want all the beings, starting with ourselves,
to be happy. ;-)
We then have greater capacity to pass on that love and happiness.
Sweet. :-)

Chapter Eighteen
Obliging and Searching for the Middle Path

"At All Places, at all times, always think of God (higher consciousness). Why are you doing a job? To look after your family. Do it with the feeling that God has given you the responsibility and you must use your resources only as much as it is necessary," said the wise man.

We as caregivers, lamplighters and friends can easily give too much. We can get drained before we realize it. Why? Because we have a big heart and we are being present, second by second, doing all we can to ease someone's discomfort, negating ourselves.

Here's a bit of wisdom we all do know, deep within our tiny being, but our larger self forgets and thinks differently. Always remember: we can only help to ease someone else's discomfort.

Please remember this fact: even if it looks like the healing was successful because the person looks and feels good, it is always temporary.

Why? Because a permanent healing or even a long lasting healing, can only be through…
Divine Interaction - Inner Action. That which is determined and created by the power of the individual and God - the big picture. Therefore, we are always the helpers, not the doers. How about that? And that is our purpose - to help.

May we have mercy on ourselves when we need it. ;-) Thank you

This world is about sharing. When we are feeling abundance is when we can easily share. Abundance comes in many forms. :-) There is the abundance of time, health, willpower, happiness, knowledge, goodwill, skills, cash - what am I forgetting?

Because we lamplighters do have many forms of abundance, we automatically help; and we need obliging skills when we need to back off to a degree, or say no, or do less, or change the help, or need to give loving discipline….

When we may be dealing with something uncomfortable or difficult,
we want to be obliging yet we do not want to oblige.
This is a challenge.

To Be
Dancing in Our Light
Is
Creating the vortex around us
Of
Compassion
Therefore, we have self loving discipline, to learn
The Art of Obliging, knowing
It is very worthwhile.

The power of differentiating thoughts from feelings, helps us to learn obliging skills.

Three examples:
A. "I feel like I can go on!"
   A more complete truth would be ... a more complete story would be...
B. "I feel happy because I now have the fortitude and perseverance to continue on!"

A. "I feel that if he does that one more time I'm going to lose it!"
B. "I am feeling angry with just the thought that he'd do that again,
   and I now realize I need to take care of business to prevent myself from losing it!

A. "I feel attacked and now I am drained. That person attacked me psychically."
B. "I am feeling actual gut-wrenching physical pain from the conflict! I (need) must allow myself
   time to heal and gather my power once more."

The above examples also show the power of personal needs and personal feelings.
My personal needs vs. someone else's needs, or their doings (actions).

A fourth example:
A. "I'm getting anxious, all this work is taking me over!"
B. "I'm feeling anxious and thinking this work is running my life!"

This example also shows differentiating 'me' as a thing, a type of label, someone who defines him/herself by their work and adopting the idea of being consumed by the state of anxiousness, as if it couldn't be controlled. Point B. is someone acknowledging being a person first by recognizing what he/she's feeling, and experiencing the overload of work. Alleluia! This is a good example of why acknowledging a feeling is important. It is saying what this human is experiencing, right now.

5 More Examples of being honest and obliging, yet standing strong when responding to something uncomfortable and possible misunderstandings.

Seeking the Middle Road

Example 1. *"Because my request to _____ has not been met, I am feeling anxious and discouraged (or vulnerable, nervous, troubled, rattled, upset, etc.). Therefore I need to change our deal. When agreements are honored, I feel respected. I need that. I love you* (or "I want the best for you") *and I'm doing all I can. Let's talk."*
VS.
"You haven't kept your end of the deal. You've been disrespecting me and you've been ditching me! You're trying to avoid the whole topic. We gotta talk!"

This example gives definition as to what is respectful to me rather than assuming, how to respect - is understood.

This next example is offering the benefit of doubt,
in order to continue a dialogue that is getting uncomfortable.
Most important!
I have love in my tone of voice and in my eyes, wanting to connect foremost!

Example 2. *"I guess I'm not speaking clearly. Let me say, this is uncomfortable, but I'm reaching for clarity and ease. Please let me try again."* ;-)

Example 3. *"I'm not liking your request, it makes me feel uncomfortable so it may sound like I'm not cooperating but my intention is to find resolution for all of us. Please, let's talk about it."*

Example 4. *"I heard through the grapevine what you said about... I know this is uncomfortable for both of us and I'd like to talk about it and find a resolution. I am here now, willing to hear you. How about you?"*

Example 5. *"Well, I've been studying some communication skills and I realize I haven't totally heard you. I want to accept all that you are and my preconceived notions have prevented my understanding of what you are dealing with. Let me hear you now, please."*

How About That?

What do we have?
Here now on
Planet Earth.

The means,
the projections
of how to
communicate?

To share our
sorrows and
joys, religiously?

That is, with
reverence
humility and
tolerance?

This is what
It is to be
Human.

Anything
less is
a miss
causing a mess.

We must
We can
Be That One
Inside each
of Us, Is
that One!

To share
To love,
Accept
Love in all
Faces.
See love
Be Love
One Love
Always here on Planet Earth!

Chapter Nineteen
Suggestions when in a situation, needing counsel.
A need to create a new vortex

The suggestion is to read through the guide and trust in an initiation into this transformation. You may want to read it again. Take your time. Repeat intriguing information. Sit with the information and allow a healing.

Review these pages:
Page 29 *"Let's check this out."*
My main question now is: *Where am I going?*
What direction am I leading my chariot?

Page 30 What am I really thinking? Becoming aware.

Study the table of Contents and make a Buddha briefcase. Use sticky tabs to tag chapters, plus pages of favorite poems and pearls of wisdom.
Tag a chapter or two that's needed right now.

A Daily Menu:
1. What am I feeling and thinking? What is my bottom-line need?

2. Make a request of myself. How may my life be enriched? What can I do?

3. When in conflict with someone.
   Ask for guidance towards soul connection, that is soul to soul.
   Then search for what they may be feeling and needing.
   Do not go to: what they are thinking?
   That may lead to creating interpretations and taking monkey mind actions.

4. Offer empathy, to yourself and to others.

*Any page may be repeated and used like a mantra, vibrating out goodwill.

Part IV

Chapter Twenty
The Embodiment of Compassion

A Sweet Story

One day I met a sweet lady in a women's group. Let's say her name was Lily. She was complaining about her job and boss. She was hoping to find a new job where she'd get more respect. Aha! I thought. So at lunch hour I decided to offer a little 'auntie' talk. I asked her if I could offer some pearls of wisdom after hearing her story in the circle. Yes, was her reply.

For a while, I listened to some of the details of Lily's job and the interaction with her boss. She needed a new boss. The present job was leading her nowhere but she did like the pay.

Sweetly, I interrupted her talk after I heard many details. Why interrupt? Several reasons.

Number 1. There is no reason, no need to repeat the story.
When someone is thinking they've been put down, until they make a conscious effort to stop, they will repeat the details over and over or tell another story with the same ending.
Repeating keeps the story alive like a mantra. It's best to stop. It's best to bring in awareness of the negating mantras. Mantras are meant to be positive. Their repetition vibrates out.

Number 2. Awareness of precious time. This time especially because we had a lunch hour.

Number 3. The possibility of getting sidetracked. Generally an upset person will have more than one agenda and can't wait to spill them all. I know. I've been there. And when I'm there, I say, *"Please shut me up, gently!"*

I presented this question:
"If you've had this job for 3 years now and you've been looking for another job, how about asking yourself, 'Why do I have this job? Why was I put here?'"

Lily was surprised. Sometimes repetition is needed. *"You have been looking for another job."* Then I added, *"You have good qualifications. I can see you are enthusiastic. Why wouldn't you be able to find another job?"*

"Yeah, right! It's been so disturbing!"

By staying there, in 'it's so disturbing' Lily is developing a type of blame.

Who is "it"?
Where are the connecting dots?
It is out there somewhere.

I asked how the boss gets along with the others. *"Oh, no one likes her."*

Without giving Lily any techniques on compassionate language tools, I offered her compassion, asking her to pass that compassion on, without ever using the word 'compassion'. She had the lamplighter switch turned on.

The compassionate light of goodwill was in her eyes. She was able to quickly process the situation with only a few questions. There was sincerity on my part to connect with her and offer pearls of wisdom.

How I had needed to get the greater picture through to her, the power of connection and the urgency to recognize her boss's pain. With our ancient eyes connecting our souls, and asking a few specific questions, I then knew deep within, I trusted her ability to process it and to get it right.

Didn't tell her to stop looking for another job. I suggested expressing appreciation for a paycheck by starting a savings account with if only a few dollars each check. Honor the work; respect herself for going to work each day, giving reverence to her God-given ability to work.

"Give that to your boss," I suggested. *"Have more direct eye contact and voice yourself. Trust yourself to be kind and offer the best you can. Turn that vortex around. See what happens."*

I saw Lily almost a year later. She was thrilled. Did she get a new job? She looked so happy. *"No,"* she said.

She began to believe that there must be a greater reason why she was there. What was God's plan?

****

I find most people believe in God. I do not hesitate to talk about God when I feel compelled. I do not use the word as a threat or leverage. But I find most people are a little hesitant to use the word. It's almost like a vulnerability word. How about that? Yet when I do use the word without the hierarchy of leverage, more like a word meaning love and tolerance, I find it opens a door to the real person. Simply adorable. How about that?

Pearl of Wisdom
No matter what name a person is using for God or Higher Consciousness,
a deep personal truth is exposed it seems,
with a bit of surprise,
the second we acknowledge together
the truth of the existence of God.

The beautiful soul then seems to pop out of the body.
Whereas after we have bonding,
ancient loving eyes of understanding
the greatest need is
to get it right.
Believing/knowing we are limited
here in time and space
and
we must reach all we can
to get it right.

At this point every person has been willing to be real, reaching out with as much authenticity and truth that can be mustered right now! Even if we must talk about death, the bearing soul is then willing. Simply adorable.

As Lily spoke I saw another side of her had developed. She had expansion in her heart. Her eyes seemed larger with the gleam of understanding the greater picture.

Lily said she had begun to appreciate her work and all of her co-workers. She hadn't thought too much about what each one had to put up with in their life. She felt compassion. And she felt compassion for her boss.

About two weeks after we first met and she had her new agenda, she was surprised that her boss asked her to lunch. Lily had no idea who her boss was until that lunch hour, even after having worked with her daily for several years. They began to share, to be real, to speak truth without any extras, no accusations, labels, guilt, etc.

The atmosphere in the office began to change. People were having better interactions. Gossip about the boss dropped. The office was becoming a welcoming home of work. Then recently, totally unexpected, she was given a bonus and offered a promotion. No, she was not presently looking for a new job.

Why did it work out so well for Lily?
Basically she had adopted the action to mimic God.
She became the embodiment of being loving and merciful. Awww.

When I met Lily in the circle, upon hearing her story, I had a great need to connect because of the connecting dots. I received the intuitive feeling that she would get the message. Not knowing exactly what I was going to say, but trusting 100% I was being guided, I allowed myself to be open to the guidance. I could feel it without doubt. Staying focused second by second while in conversation with Lily allowed the message to flow with ease. Awww.

Owning the Choice to Hear
There is freedom in one's mind and heart
toward a field of expansion and fun curiosity,
when allowed
the processing
to begin with owning the choice to hear.

It is important then, to ask if pearls of wisdom may be offered.

Yes Yes!

Yes yes! He says	Doer
Mission accomplished	Do here
Words of Wisdom	Do now
Passed on.	Do you hear?
Open hearts may see	Can you now
The Guidance	Bear witness
Presented….	to letting Go
Then destiny has it!	and See
God then steps in	the growing
and	whirlwind of love
Continues the story.	and joy
Ha Ha	circulating the vortex
He alone	of goodwill and harmony.
That destiny	God's gift to you then,
Bearer	on auto.

Chapter Twenty-One
Let's Talk About Love

La Chirimoya Metals

As a young adult I fell into a career where I made custom jewelry.

After a while it became apparent to me that all people need the very same thing: acceptance. This was odd to me. People from around the world and all walks of life came into our little shop. They were so completely different from each other. These folks had their own quests in life. Rarely did they cross paths. Yet they were all engaged in the same need, acceptance.

The odd part was their fear of non-acceptance.
I could sense it.
I could feel the connecting dots although I did not know they existed.

It was a beautiful shop with 12 foot brick walls to decorate. It was enjoyable to visit. People would stay a while. A regular comment was that it looked more like a museum.

The career opened up to a type of counseling career for me. My main income came from wedding rings. Since they were custom made, the variation of styles was endless. Rarely did couples know what they wanted, so I'd ask, *"What brought you together?"* My desire was that they create a design that meant something to them.

Little did I know the question presented them with space to think, share and define themselves to each other. It gave them sacred space. They'd go home, and come back with stories and ideas. We'd talk, I'd observe and listen. Something was brewing. Since I was young and naïve, I had no idea I was helping to connect dots. Sometimes an aggravation would come up and I'd think, *"Why did I go there? Now I've lost a customer."* But I hadn't. They'd come back looking even more in love.

After several years I began to understand I was actually helping a process. Many of the couples who sought my work had been together for years and finally had the desire to seal the deal. I thought that was odd, too.

How could a long-time couple still need help? At times our dialogue would be somewhat detailed. And how could they benefit from such a young person, me? What did I know?

What I didn't know
is how much people need acceptance and how much it is questioned.

Acceptance Acceptance Acceptance
with Passion

This is what seemed to be achieved by the time the rings were finished.

We had an artist guild co-op. There were five jewelers and one oil painter who were the heart of the shop, plus artistic friends and lovers. A few determined members defined the decor and ambience of the shop. Thus the museum look with fine modern art, unique artifacts and antiques from Europe and Tibet.

Therefore, I could understand the hesitation when someone entered. The 12 foot ceilings allowed large paintings and items, many odd and beautiful. Customers needed reassurance to enter our little big shop. It seemed small because of the size of the two outdoor display windows. Then with a textured copper door sitting center, you'd enter into a large space with high old red walls, massive paintings and items here and there, plus five handmade jewelry display tables.

**As the years rolled by I was taught the universal need for acceptance.
It seems to be a constant need for most everyone.**

Not only did the couples need reassurance. Little by little I would come to recognize a look each person had as they interacted with the other. The look showed the need for assurance and acceptance. I could understand why the look was there with me, a stranger in a strange place. But, like the couples, folks seemed to be on the same quest across the board: a quest for acceptance from the members of their group. Each member had the look to a degree, some more than others.

It did not matter how much money they had, or what they bought or didn't buy. All folks were looking for the same thing, acceptance. What I did not know was that the underlying need was to be heard.

This is a Big Deal!
When someone thinks they have been heard
with completeness,

*it means they have the satisfaction of
being understood.*

*Being understood
brings in a sense of deep love from another.*

Acceptance. Awww :-)

*In all my years of various counseling I'd say there is a great need and there is a great lack --
that of being heard.*

*Therefore acceptance is constantly sought. That, I did not understand for a long, long time.
How about that.*

*These are my pearls of wisdom for you,
dear lamplighter.*

In summary...

By entering the realm... the vortex... the influence... the warmth... the love of the Art of Compassionate Language, that is: the Art of Wanting to Choose Words for a Compassionate Conversation, with ourselves and with all others, we may consciously, majestically and magically create a fruitful loving life.

By creating loving and merciful discipline with ourselves
we are
Dancing Through Our Light,
continuously creating
Compassion,
whirling and transforming,
a life where,
compassion more and more may become our norm.
Hallelujah!

It is the desire to connect soul to soul and hear what is going on in this life.
Yes!!!

This is.... the journey of compassion.

It creates a spiritual life full of love, offering and attracting love.

*We then live joyously promoting peace,
harmony and the desire to understand each other
soul to soul!*

Chapter Twenty-Two
a little truth

The mind is only a tool, just like money.

The solar system moves around and around and so does our mind.

Thoughts go in and out, none are permanent just as the solar system cannot stay in a permanent state, position, it must move on.

So even if one dwells on a topic, each thought, each word is still fresh.

By letting the stream of words come forth you may seek a deeper self, that of allowing!

The babbling goes on and on only to seek comfort.

Only when the stream is allowed to babble out of the river with force does the water feed the terrain.

inspired 5-5-2016 @ 5 a.m.

Part V

Chapter Twenty-Three
A Lamplighter's Guide to Soul Communication

**The gateway to communicating with our soul is by acknowledging what we are feeling.
Then we talk to our deepest self.**

When you finish reading this how-to book, all the way through,
I invite you to do the **Soul Journey.**

Because we have an indigenous need to be loving and merciful,
working with the included list of feelings,
is a soul journey that I guarantee will be very worthwhile!

Let's do a simple exercise to recognize the difference between feelings.

Right now, for a quick exercise:
sit for a couple of seconds with the intention
to capture our early memory ability of simply sitting and feeling.

Take your time.
Recognize hearing.
Do not ask yourself, *"What am I hearing?"*
Allow sound to simply travel.

***

Now that you have a glimpse of that particular sense of sound traveling through.....
No words attached, or the sense of just being and sound being....

Think gratitude.
"I feel grateful."

Now think satisfied.
"I feel satisfied."

Recognize how you were able to differentiate and feel each emotion.
This is a fun process now and then to build up a vocabulary of just feeling words.

This Soul Journey is what our soul wants to talk about

We are talking about a journey into another sphere, another dimension.
A place that takes us to a deep, deep, loving and truthful conversation.

Our Soul Journey is like a crystal path
into recognizing and simplifying what we are actually feeling,
who we are actually being.
Therefore we need to differentiate it from any other thoughts.

This will help us to unscramble feelings that jam us up.

We use our mind to have a conversation
with our soul and persona (ego) through our emotions and needs. Yes!

****

**To allow myself
to know the variety of emotions going through my mind and body,
releases waves of deep understanding and empathy.
This gives me freedom and expansion!**

A Little Story.

One day after a tragic event I decided to look up the list, to see if it could help me to get the day going. My happiness had vanished. My gut felt somewhat wrenched. It can be easy for me to go there.

Quickly I identified the feelings of maybe 5-6 words, admitting I owned them. I felt them! As I continued to look over the list, I began to feel a little smile as I realized I did not feel all those other words! I did not own them, not even a tad!

When the gut feels wrenched, it is all-consuming, so my drama queen wanted to think I was feeling all of it, every single sad emotion!! But there were only a handful of emotions going through me!

I could then sit with those feelings, and allow God (Higher Consciousness) to do His trick. I said, *"Let's talk about these emotions, strongly felt, right now, honestly, courageously. Thank you."*

A little later I said, *"Give me an answer as to what is my bottom line, thought or action that I need to release this sad emotion. How can it be surrendered, so I may go on with my day? How can I release it to God's hands?"* It felt uplifting just to know God was listening. I gave myself, my ego the consoling it needed. The consoling I needed. I was being motherly and fatherly to my own self. And it felt good. It felt soothing. Eventually I felt grateful and sympathetic to my own self.

After a while, while looking at the list of feelings from unmet needs, :-(though I still felt sadness and needed to deal with heavy conditions, I was pleased to recognize some feelings that I had felt other times but that I did not own now.

I had grown. I felt a type of inner balance, knowing I was now more equipped to handle life and tribulations. This fact gave me encouragement. I then finished with the happy list :-)

Going over the happy :-) list gave me more encouragement. Acknowledging my sadness, gathering up my inner happiness, I was then able to get on with the day, better equipped to pass on the empathy that I had just given myself. Awww.

I pray today

I pray today
dear Lord
I may seek
an understanding,

An understanding
of who I may
want to be.

Upon discovering
true, all that I feel
may I tap now
into that soul

Soul who's always
questioning me.
Can I be me?
Who am I?
Is there more?

May I know today
at least
my soul's
feeling.

Today?
What emotions
did I play?

Steps to Our Soul Journey

Listed here are many words to describe feelings.
They are separated into two categories: when needs are met, and when needs are not met.

* Start with the list of words that describe when needs are not being met.
***Always** finish with the list of words that describe when needs are being met.

Feelings going on inside right now……… what are they?

Or a past story, what feelings did my mind and body experience?
What did I feel back then?

> ***We may heal our past and present wounds by consoling ourselves now.***
> We can extract the painful emotions out of our being,
> those that are somewhere in our body and chakra energy field.

> ***We do this through our love and true self empathy.***
> Hearing with honesty and accepting our deepest self through our emotions,
> we can finally let it go,
> splashing its last essence upon the sands of eternity.

> We may then fill ourselves up with our preferred emotions.
> Just like the Buddha. We'd then be in the zen, hehe.
> Thank you and hallelujah!
> Emotions that I wanna feel, about myself and towards another.

***

"My Dear Lord, allow me to hear myself with understanding. Help me to experience these emotions with confidence, knowing that I AM capable of feeding my soul and healing my wounds, releasing waves of stored emotions. Allow me to feel the real me, and may the joy, power and strength of your love and perseverance, surface."

A list of some emotions that we feel when our needs are being met. :-)

Affectionate
compassionate
friendly
loving
open hearted
sympathetic
tender
warm

Confident
brave
courageous
empowered
open
proud
safe
secure

Engaged
absorbed
alert
curious
dreamy
engrossed
enchanted
entranced
fascinated
interested
intrigued
involved
spellbound
stimulated
valued

Excited
amazed
animated
aroused
astonished
dazzled
eager

energetic
enthusiastic
giddy
invigorated
lively
passionate
surprised
vibrant

Exhilarated
blissful
ecstatic
effervescent
elated
enthralled
exuberant
radiant
rapturous
thrilled

Grateful
appreciative
moved
thankful
touched

Hopeful
expectant
encouraged
optimistic

Inspired
amazed
awed
sympathetic
wonder

Joyful
amused
delighted
glad

good
happy
jubilant
pleased
tickled

Peaceful
calm
clear-headed
comfortable
centered
content
equanimous
fulfilled
good
mellow
quiet
relaxed
relieved
satisfied
serene
still
tranquil
trusting

Refreshed
fresh
rejuvenated
renewed
rested
restored
uplifted

Some emotions we feel when our needs are not being met :-(

Agony
anguished
bereaved
devastated
disheartened
grief
hurt
lonely
miserable
mournful
pain
regretful
woe

Afraid
apprehensive
alarmed
dread
foreboding
fearful
frightened
guarded
leery
mistrustful
nervous
panicked
panicky
petrified
scared
suspicious
terrified
wary
worried

Angry
enraged
furious
incensed
indignant
irate
livid
outraged
resentful

Annoyed
aggravated
agitated
discombobulated
disturbed
displeased
exasperated
frustrated
impatient
irritated
perturbed
rattled
restless
shocked
startled
troubled
turmoil
uncomfortable
unsettled
upset

Aversion
animosity
appalled
contempt
disgusted
dislike
hate
horrified
hostile
repulsed
resentful

resentment
Confused
ambivalent
baffled
bewildered
conflicted
dazed
doubtful
hesitant
lost
mystified
perplexed
puzzled
torn
unsure

Disconnected
alienated
aloof
apathetic
bored
cold
contemptuous
detached
discouraged
distant
distracted
indifferent
inhibited
numb
nonchalant
passive
removed
reserved
unconcerned
uninterested
withdrawn

Cont'd ;-(list

Embarrassed
ashamed
flustered
guilty
mortified
regretful
remorseful
self-conscious
shy
sorry

Sad
bad
depressed
dejected
despair
despondent
disappointed
discouraged
dissatisfied
gloomy
heavy
hearted
hopeless
melancholy
unhappy
wretched

Tired
beat
bored
burnt out
depleted
exhausted
fatigue
lethargic
listless
sleepy
tired
weary
worn out

Tense
anxious
constricted
cranky
distressed
distraught
edgy
fidgety
frazzled
intense
irritable
jittery
nervous
overwhelmed
restless
stressed

Vulnerable
fragile
guarded
helpless
insecure
leery
reserved
sensitive
shy

Yearning
desirous
envious
jealous
longing
nostalgic
pining
wistful

Acknowledgements

With barely knowing how to read and write, finally, after much hard work, I went to college!

There they told me I needed to take a remedial reading and writing course again! And if I agreed I could also take a college course in English literature. Thrilled, I didn't know what that meant except that I could now claim I was taking a college course!

Our professor was an Old English Gent.

We were required to read and then write an essay about what we read using some rules he invented. No more memorizing sentence structure and facts about this nor that which I cared nothing about.

I was thrilled but the other students were not. To me his rules were a type of logic but the other students now had to think and express themselves in a different manner. There was no guarantee of a grade A with only knowing their familiar memorized facts. Facts like if a word was spelled correctly or used in proper sentence structure. He did not care. I was relieved.

My father had promised me a time when I could use my mind once I was grown. I heard my professor say,
"You're grown up now, what do you have to say, what's on your mind?"

My success in class produced the only college course where I did receive an actual A-grade. There were only a few of us with that gold star of an A- grade.

Upon attempting to write this book, feeling weak, knowing my inabilities, I remembered the kind English Professor who on my last paper wrote me a note. He said that I had the ability to express my feelings and that it would lead me to my success in life.

I did not understand him at the time. It made no sense, except that he thought I would have success. Thank you dear sir, wherever you are, for believing in me. No one had ever said anything like that to me before!

His words kept me going, giving me some thoughts that just maybe I'll be understood and help someone somewhere with this work. And so I kept writing and writing, his words encouraging me continuously. This way the old English gent has continued to mentor me and I thank him. A good teacher is precious! Encouragement is sacred to me.

To my spiritual Guru, the Head Honcho-God, who has proved beyond a shadow of a doubt that He's got my back, I am in deep gratitude for the guidance to write.

And to all my Divine Friends, I thank you so much for your patience with me, sitting there on the sidelines, encouraging inspiration.

I'd also like to thank Marilyn Kapp, who's been so much fun with our 5 hour luncheons and discussions on, 'how to save the world!' Plus the giggles and insights, a treasure always.

To my courageous brother, Victor Villaseñor, for having persevered through over 50 years of public writing, who is now my studious writing teacher, thank you.

To my sister, Linda Villaseñor who has loved and encouraged me all the way! Thank you.

Also many thanks to Maribeth Bandas, my editor who can help interpret my scrambled-up concepts. Thank you.

Thank you to Hillary Sunenshine for the beautiful book cover.

Thank you to Alexander Kohnke, Artist and Master Designer, thank you for your patience in the ever changing typesetting needed to create this book.

I'd also like to thank Bill Gladstone, my brother's agent who loves him and so quickly said yes! yes! let's publish this work!

Thank you to all my sava-dal friends for their lifelong work of encouraging my spirit and our connections!

To Stephanie O'Riely, my friend who stepped up and suggested we start a Lamplighters study group, thank you and for all your attention, intuition, love and encouragement, forever grateful.

A special round of thanks to our first table of Lamplighters who have shared their wealth of knowledge in refining this guide: Stephanie O'Riely, Marilyn Kapp, Jenna Shulman, Maribeth Bandas, Phyllis Wohlberg, Michelle Miler, Kim Jefferson, Vanessa Graziano, Cathy Patrick, Hillary Sunenshine, Karsyn Lee, Glenna Davis

A Passion for Compassion

Author's Papá, Sal Villaseñor on his beloved horse, Cherokee, 1959

Sita Paloma

Author's Mamá, Lupe Villaseñor, 1929

Author's Childhood home
Hacienda built by her father, designed by her mother, 1952

Author's Debut as Dancer, age 7

Testimonials

"I'm so proud of my little sister. Her new book starts out with 'My wish to write a lullaby.' Well what is a lullaby? It's not a lecture. It's not a bossy how to do book. A lullaby is a gentle loving way of sharing feelings. By the end of this book you're going to feel understood, validated, and realize that when we speak to each other with the feelings of a lullaby, arguments and disagreements disappear, because we are centered in compassion, empathy, and therefore are able to glimpse the good each other's heart and soul." Victor Villasenor, Best selling author, Rain of Gold.

"To know Sita is to know magic. But not just any magic. She is a reminder of the magic that each and every one of us carries inside. Sometimes we just need to be reminded that it's there, that it is a constant, whether we're aware of it or not. She shares a lullaby. A lullaby to wake us up! A lullaby to carry us beyond the rest and slumber, to the place where we open our eyes….. and mind…. and heart…. where are individual journey connects with the light in all of us. Sita rocks us awake. The sweetness is contagious. And I'm grateful. I believe you will be, too." Marilyn Kapp, Medium to the Stars and author, Love is Greater Then Pain.

"Becoming a Lamplighter has been both a gift and a blessing, something that has expanded my heart as well as my perspective. This beautiful manuscript is something I can refer to when in doubt, a reminder of potential compassionate choice, a guide book for continued growth through our Collective Evolution and a reflection of a new paradigm living. Thank you for showing us the way to live through Love!" Jenna Schulman, MA Consciousness Studies

"There's Hope! learning how to get to Freedom. freedom from reacting to a situation instead of delving into your feelings behind it." Linda Villasenor, Editor and Sita Paloma's sister

"From a heart filled with love and compassion, Sita empowers us to stop, be fully on our Path and stay present in our lives with her own 'human stories'; from challenge to spiritual growth. How about that!" Toby Johnson, HHP

"Allow Sita Palomas wisdom and Whimsy to lead you into a world of compassion and personal growth. her Pearls of Wisdom poetry and stories hold joy and passion, nuggets of Brilliance and blessings. and she leads us through her journey towards a passion for compassion, the tapestry of her writing gives us Sparks of resonance that allow us to grow along with her. I am honored to have walked with her on the journey to bring this book to fruition." Maribeth Bandas, MA, MPil, Translator English/Spanish

"A Passion for Compassion By Dancing Through Our Light' is a lovely road map for anyone who wants to begin a healing journey, learning the necessary tools to become more compassionate with yourself and others. It led me to a path of healing so that my heart was expanded to support my mother with compassion when we both needed it the most when she was in hospice care. I will be forever grateful to have had sita's beautiful words stories and examples to help me at such a tender time. Cathy Patrick, Sound Healer

"A beautiful guide to connection and empathy, Paloma shares an inspiring wondrous method for community care and emotional healing, bringing us closer to those that are most important to us." Hillary Sunenshine, Mystical Messenger, Designer and Poet

"Reading this book, 'A Passion for Compassion' is like being in a live conversation with a friend. a wise woman who shares Life Experiences, observations and possibilities. Using antidotes, metaphors, analogies and good ol common sense, everyday solutions/ explanations are explored and simplified. Giving the reader practical 'how to's do's' to navigate life's adventure and challenges. Highly recommend Visiting this Friend!" Sylvia Aurora, Inner World Music

"After reading, breathing and practicing the techniques taught in 'A Passion for Compassion', I began to recognize the transformation I was going through. I was really hearing not only the words but the feelings people were sharing with me in conversation. I began to see into their souls rather than just the surface of their words. And in doing so, I have become a more loving, compassionate and supportive person, providing greater meaning and service with each conversation I engage in. Thank you Sita Paloma for sharing. This God inspired information has enchanted and expanded my Lamplighter Journey." Michelle V Miller, Independent Living instructor for California Department of Social Services

"Reading 'A Passion for Compassion by Dancing Through Our Light, a Lamplighter's Guide' was a transformative experience that truly touched my heart and soul. This incredible manuscript weaves together the profound themes of compassion, empathy, and unity in a way that is both enlightening and inspiring. The author's ability to bring people together through the power of words is truly remarkable. By creating a space for individuals to connect,, and open their hearts to one another, this manuscript serves as a beacon of light in a world that often feels divided. What struck me most about this manuscript was how seemingly it guided me through its pages, effortlessly leading me on a journey of self-discovery and reflection. The writers creativity in crafting a narrative of healing, love, and understanding is nothing short of genius. Through 'A Passion for Compassion' I have learned the importance of embracing our shared humanity and cultivating a deep sense of oneness and consciousness. This manuscript has the power to ignite a spark within each reader, encouraging us to shine brightly as Lamplighters in our own communities. I wholeheartedly recommend 'A Passion for Compassion' to anyone seeking to explore the depths of their own compassion and empathy. It is a masterpiece that has the potential to bring about positive change in the world, one open heart at a time." Vanessa Graziano, certified spiritual psychologist/E4-Trauma, SUD counselor

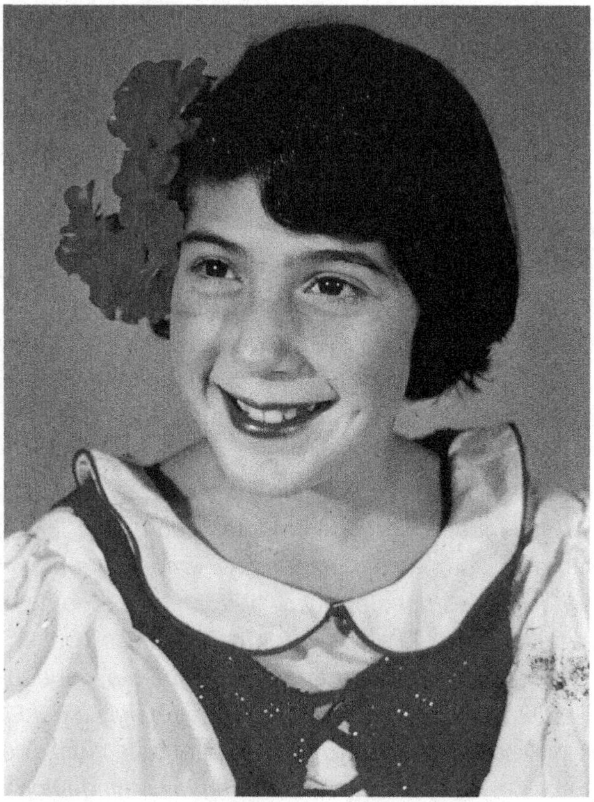

Made in the USA
Las Vegas, NV
08 June 2025